Also by Aerial Cross

Ants in Their Pants: Teaching Children Who Must Move to Learn

COME AND PLAY

Sensory-Integration Strategies for Children
with Play Challenges

AERIAL CROSS

Redleaf Press®
www.redleafpress.org
800-423-8309

Published by Redleaf Press
10 Yorkton Court
St. Paul, MN 55117
www.redleafpress.org

First edition 2010
Cover design by Elizabeth Berry
Interior typeset in Berkeley and Futura and designed by Jim Handrigan
Interior illustrations by Todd Balthazor
Printed in the United States of America
17 16 15 14 13 12 11 10   1 2 3 4 5 6 7 8

This book contains names of numerous products and the companies that produce them. Neither the author nor Redleaf Press endorses or sells any of the products mentioned, and neither is affiliated with any of the businesses that produce them. Redleaf Press is not responsible for any dissatisfaction you may experience with any of the products or businesses referred to herein.

Library of Congress Cataloging-in-Publication Data
Cross, Aerial.
  Come and play : sensory-integration strategies for children with play challenges / Aerial Cross.
  p. cm.
  Includes bibliographical references.
  ISBN 978-1-60554-022-1 (alk. paper)
  1. Play. 2. Early childhood education. 3. Sensorimotor integration. 4. Child development. I. Title.
  LB1139.35.P55C76 2010
  155.42'3—dc22
                        2010017227

TO MY FATHER—I MISS YOU

Contents

Acknowledgments

Thank you to PJ, Farrah, and Bella—you continue to amaze me.

Thanks to my students—you teach me!

And thanks to Eileen, Michelle, and Shawn—the power of girlfriends!

The beginning is the most important part of any work, especially in the case of a young and tender thing.

—Plato

An Introduction to Sensory-Integration Strategies for Play Challenges

As a child care provider or educator, you play a tremendous role in the life of children. You have the power to offer a child miraculous gifts on a daily basis—opportunities for a happy, healthy, and productive life. By far the most influential gift you'll present to a young child is a healthy concept of play, including how to be successful at play with peers. Healthy play is an integral part of a child's growth and development. It

- enhances a child's dexterity

- promotes social skills

- sharpens cognitive and language skills

- encourages spatial understanding

- develops cause-and-effect reasoning

- clarifies pretend and real

- enriches sensory and aesthetic appreciation

- extends attention span, play persistence, and self-mastery
- helps release emotions

(Honig 2007, 72–78)

Healthy childhood play is joyful and motivational to watch. Productive and healthy childhood play is ever extending, reaching intensely into make-believe processes. It typically resembles children entering play eagerly, taking turns, and communicating with peers to negotiate and compromise when conflict presents itself. Interaction with peers in play is cooperative. Peer role-playing and pretending with creative materials and concrete objects unfolds smoothly. Children engaged in healthy play are interested and excited during routine daily activities, such as circle time and story time. Healthy childhood play typically resembles the following examples:

- John taking turns at a learning center and communicating to his peers when his turn has been overlooked.

- Kelly engaged during center time, not wandering about the classroom.

- Amy excited to participate in peer play.

- Charley eagerly entering a play area and interacting with his peers.

- Kate cooperatively role-playing and pretending with creative materials and concrete objects with her peers.

Healthy childhood play does not typically resemble the following examples:

- John puttering at a learning center and not communicating to his peers when his turn has been overlooked. John is dabbling.

- Kelly meandering around the classroom during afternoon playtime. Kelly is roaming.

- Amy reluctant and hesitant to participate in peer play. Amy appears anxious.

- Charley standing nervously at the edge of a play area and avoiding interaction with his peers. Charley appears detached.

- Kate roughly role-playing and pretending with creative materials and concrete objects with her peers and hitting a playmate when not given what she wants. Kate is risking rejection from her peers.

No matter the type—constructive, outdoor, physical, or cooperative—play helps children learn and developmentally thrive, and the health and productivity of a child's play greatly affects later learning. Today many young children wrestle with issues of discipline, academic learning, and social interaction, struggles that are often rooted in play challenges. Play challenges can manifest anywhere along the play-stage progression (the three stages of play) and can limit the development of needed skills, causing stagnant, personality-less play. Stagnant play without personality can cause problems, especially to a child's social, emotional, physical, linguistic, and cognitive development. Fortunately, play challenges can be tackled early on.

"Young children who receive quality early intervention have a greater probability of succeeding in school and in life" (Isbell and Isbell 2007, 48). Early intervention for play challenges by parents, grandparents, educators, social workers, counselors, Sunday school teachers, speech therapists, physical therapists, occupational therapists, and child care professionals—those fortunate to be part of young children's magical world of play—is essential.

Play Challenges

A play challenge is a breakdown or severe stagnation in a child's ability to progress through developmentally appropriate stages of play in relation to individual growth and development. When a child fails to consistently play with ease, naturalness, and intrinsic motivation; to consistently interact with age-appropriate peers; or to consistently engage with presented play materials, a play challenge is present.

Here are five common play challenges that limit a child's play potential and developmental skill acquisition:

- repetitious dabbling during play

- continual roaming around the playroom

- continual anxiousness about or during play

- continual detachment or unfriendliness during play

- continual rejection by playmates during play

When a play challenge has been observed over a consistent and patterned period of time and impedes or prevents a child from developing in any major skill-acquisition process, such as healthy social interaction with peers, or in an area of development, such as emotional growth, intervention by the educator is needed.

Intervention is the initiation of work to address a child's play challenge by improving play performance affecting major developmental areas, such as academic, social, emotional, and physical growth. Early intervention strategies may include taking daily anecdotal notes or keeping logs, developing an individual play plan (see appendix B), play tutoring, or conferencing with a parent or guardian to begin devising possible play challenge solutions. With early intervention, play challenges can be corrected and redirected, sparing the development of discipline issues (such as continual disruptive classroom behavior) and the labeling that can stem from the identification of the play challenge itself. A child who feels labeled, or set apart from her peers, may suffer emotionally. Use the early intervention strategies provided in this book. When you observe worsening play behavior patterns, document the cause and effect. For example, when Beth's mother drops her off at school in the morning, she hesitates in her departure, and Beth becomes clingy and withdrawn after her mother leaves. In consultation with others in the child's network (a parent and a therapist, for example), implement the sensory-integration play strategies you'll encounter in coming chapters.

A child's uniqueness affects her play. It is, therefore, imperative to understand, identify, and respect a child's individual nature and approaches to learning and developing. Consider the child's nature, personality, peculiarities, home life, and eating and sleeping habits when answering the question, "What is, or could be, the root cause of this play challenge?" Keep a journal to track a child's patterns of play behaviors. Ongoing logging may confirm hunches about or exclude possibilities for the root cause of a play challenge, as well as identify classroom practices and strategies that are or are not working for the child.

Sometimes the root cause of a play challenge is simple and easily overlooked. For example, a child may dabble and appear detached during circle time—simply because he is not a morning person. He may simply need time to wake up and get going. To accommodate such a child, the teacher could implement creative and upbeat morning stretches during circle time or extend circle time by five to ten minutes with a movement activity, such as a high-energy version of Simon Says.

Other times the root cause is not simple and something deep down is wrong. For example, a teacher discerns that a child is consistently demonstrating sudden and noticeable anxiety during circle time. After a meeting with her mother, the teacher discovers the child's parents are in the midst of a heated divorce, which could be the root cause of the sudden anxious behavior. A possible accommodation to aid the child's play performance could be to implement with her parents a consistent schedule at both of the homes in which the child resides. The home schedules could temporarily resemble the school schedule as closely as possible. For example, lunch could be served at the same time as it is at school and could be eaten with the parent. This would provide the child with a sense of stability and consistency, which might alleviate her anxiety. Though you may be tempted to do so, don't apply a quick fix to a complex play problem. Seek out the root cause of the play challenge instead.

When working with children who consistently dabble, wander, appear detached or anxious, or are rejected during play, think creatively—outside the box. Don't be afraid to get messy, silly, and loud with children. As long as children are learning, thriving, and smiling, don't worry what the teacher next door might be thinking. Shoot for recognizable yet fresh, imaginative, stimulating, and purposeful activities to address play challenges, such as the following:

- outdoor painting on easels or tree stumps with an assortment of paints, brushes, and background music

- fancy feet washing, in which children remove their shoes and socks, wash their feet in large tubs of warm, soapy water, and then dry them off with fluffy towels and draw faces on their toes with washable markers

- snacking on sliced bananas painted on by the children with fine paintbrushes and a variety of colored and thinly watered-down Jell-O powders

In the early years, a child's intrinsic motivation to learn is largely based on curiosity, hands-on investigation, and creative self-expression. Each is an integral part of the learning that helps build a child's sense of competence, which assists in overcoming play challenges. Each is developmentally appropriate for effective learning. Developmentally appropriate practices (DAP) are planned content and strategies for creatively educating students that take into account everything known about how children develop and learn. Keeping play challenge strategies aligned with emotional and social development standards and developmentally appropriate practices is important. For further reading on DAP, consult these resources:

Developmentally Appropriate Practice in Early Childhood Programs Serving Children Birth through Age 8 by Carol Copple and Sue Bredekamp

Successfully Moving toward Developmentally Appropriate Practice: It Takes Time and Effort! by Judith L. Vander Wilt and Virginia Monroe

Remember to do what is in the best interest of the child's growth and development, not what is most convenient or easily scheduled into a district's scripted curriculum. Refer to early childhood social and emotional development standards when investigating play challenge patterns of behavior and concerns, and use logical deduction to understand the play challenge. As in the game of Clue, everyone (everything) is suspect.

The Stages of Play and Learning Development

As an educator and blessed mother of three, I've come to understand four powerful pieces of information about play:

1. Children who find play enjoyable will sustain it, seek more of it, improve on it, and ultimately learn from it.

2. Anna Freud, daughter of Sigmund, accurately stated, "Play is the work of children." Play is a powerfully significant part of a child's life and should be well supported by parents and educators.

3. For optimal development, children require a menu of substantial amounts of time, space, creative materials, and open-ended experiences for healthy and quality play. It is the job of parents and educators to serve up and set a magical stage for fruitful play.

4. Play has distinct characteristics and progressive stages, all of which are necessary milestones in a child's development.

Children approach and discover the world most comfortably through play and progress naturally, if not differently, through the stages of play in unique and individual ways. Some children thrive on imaginative and quiet constructive play. Some children require constant conversation with peers during play, while competition or exploratory play drives others. Many people who are actively and regularly engaged with children agree that a strong connection exists between a child's early play and developmental learning later on.

There are three stages of play. During the first stage, solitary play (which occurs from birth through the toddler years), children play alone with toys, their hands and feet, or any other object of interest. During the second stage, parallel play (starting after toddlerhood until around three years of age), children begin to play standing or sitting next to one another without necessarily playing with each other—though their awareness of each other is sprouting. During the third stage, cooperative play (from three years of age and up), children begin interacting with each other. They begin learning to share, take turns, communicate, negotiate, compromise, and observe obvious differences between themselves and others.

Fred Rogers said, "I believe that everything in a child's development is connected—what has gone before, what is happening now, and what will happen in the future" (Laney 2005, 187). Stages of play and learning development are interrelated. When considering if a child has a play challenge, which can occur during any stage of play, identify the stage of play the child is in by looking closely at each stage and how the child interacts with peers. For example, during the third stage, cooperative play (from three years of age and up), children begin interacting with each other in several ways. When pondering how the child developmentally entered the stage, ask yourself, "Did the child enter this stage willing and eager to share, take turns, communicate, negotiate, and compromise? Or was the child reluctant to do these things and in need of continual prompting to make progress in the cooperative play stage?"

An acronym that helps gather information about a child's play and learning development is PLEAS C ME. (Think of a child entering the classroom for the first time, with arms open wide, expressing, "Please see me!") The acronym represents areas and components of a child's play, learning, and growth development— P (physical), L (language), E (emotional), A (adaptive), S (social),

C (cognitive), M (motor), and E (eight multiple intelligences)—and is helpful in identifying a child's stage of play. The acronym helps a teacher or caregiver observe patterns of play that may not align with a play stage, and it pinpoints major areas of a young child's development as each stage of play is entered and exited. Use the acronym as the foundation for observation. Based on the areas and components of a child's play, learning, and the growth development it represents, record specifically targeted anecdotal loggings to discern patterns of a possible play challenge.

For example, during the second stage, parallel play (starting after toddlerhood until around three years of age), children begin to play standing or sitting next to each other without necessarily playing with each other—though their awareness of each other is developing. If a wandering play challenge begins to unravel within a child during the parallel play stage, and if on reviewing acronym notes about the child it's clear that developmentally and individually the child is on track in all areas except "S" (social), then the child's social development might be a target for intervention.

P = **Physical.** Consider the child's physical development, which involves bodily change and growth (Essa and Rogers 1992, 23). "Physical" includes observance of any physical disabilities, disorders, or delays in the child's appearance and growth.

- Is the child's vision poor (does she wear glasses)?

- Is the child hard of hearing (does he wear a hearing aid)?

- Does the child have any obvious orthopedic disability (is she wheelchair bound with limited use of her arms and legs)?

- Does the child have an Individualized Education Program (IEP) for a specific physical disability or disorder?

- Does the child have an obvious delay in physical growth or development (is he very small for his age)?

L = **Language.** A child's ability to communicate with peers is important and directly affects areas of social, emotional, and cognitive development. "Language" includes the development of the child's communication, speech, and language skills.

- Does the child stutter, slur words, or have a lisp?

- Is the child's pronunciation of letter sounds intelligible?

- Is the child bilingual or an English-language learner?

- Does the child use sign language?

- How are the child's overall communication and speaking skills?

- Does the child use gestures in place of language?

- Does the child have frequent outbursts caused by communication frustration?

- How is the child's conversational tone, volume, and vocabulary usage?

E = Emotional. Children are more successful formulating peer play relationships when they are able to control their emotions and respond to others' emotions with kindness, patience, and cooperation. "Emotional" includes the development of the child's emotions and maturation.

- Is the child more or less emotionally mature than her peers?

- How well can the child control his behaviors?

- How does the child present herself when interacting with peers in play?

- How does the child act when he is frustrated?

- During play, does the child listen to her peers or do her own thing?

- Does the child follow directions and play as a member of the team?

- How polite is the child during play?

A = Adaptive. A child's ability to alter, bend, and blend as situations arise is dependent on how effectively and quickly the child can adapt to the situation. Some children adapt with ease. Others require more time and coaxing. "Adaptive" includes the child's ability to adjust to changes in activities, practices, the environment, and materials and encompasses transitioning.

- Does the child work well with peers to formulate a variety of play activity responses?

- Do the child's functional skills—skills the child uses to successfully complete his day, such as brushing his teeth, preparing a simple snack, zipping up his coat, tying his shoe, or reading a restroom sign for "Boys"—need to be addressed before he performs, plays, or learns a new activity?

- How does the child respond to repetition and specific sequencing or tasks that have been broken down into steps?

- Is it difficult for the child to transition from one activity to another or to switch modes of learning?

- Does the child cry or display temper during transitions?

S = Social. A child's social skills directly affect success in education. When a child struggles to control emotions or to follow classroom rules and interact with peers, the quality of social play experiences dwindles. "Social" includes the development of the child's social skills.

- How does the child play with peers and interact with adults?

- Does the child have obvious deficits in social skills?

- Does the child exert self-control when flustered?

- Does the child listen?

- Does the child read nonverbal-language cues?

C = Cognitive. Research shows that other areas of a child's development go hand in hand with cognitive growth (Marcon 2003, 80). "Cognitive" includes the development of the child's school-readiness and academic skills.

- Where is the child in regard to cognitive standards for language, math, and writing skills?

- Does the child repeat ineffective patterns, such as failing to use one-to-one correspondence when counting?

- Is the child bored with an activity because it lacks a creative, physical, or cognitive challenge?

M = Motor. Children need to learn basic motor skills, such as jumping, skipping, hopping, and balancing. Children also require strength to participate fully in classroom activities from cutting paper to playing a game of tug-of-war. The child's acquisition of fine- and gross-motor skills is important to educational progress. Without a variety of activities to practice such skills, a child's motor development will suffer.

"Motor" includes the development of a child's gross- and fine-motor skills and encompasses such aspects as muscle tone, strength, movement quality and range, eye-hand coordination, and motor planning, or the ability to do physical things in sequence (Biel and Peske 2005, 22).

- Does the child have high (tight) or low (loose) muscle tone?

- How strong are the child's muscles? How much pressure can the child's body withstand? What is the child's posture like?

- Are the child's physical movements jerky, rigid, smooth, slow, or fast?

- Can the child make movements that span the entire length of the body?

- Can the child successfully cut paper into strips or string simple beads?

- Can the child hold both feet together, jump, and land with both feet together (Biel and Peske 2005, 22)?

E = Eight Multiple Intelligences. Consider Howard Gardner's eight multiple intelligences when evaluating the child. These eight multiple intelligences are

- Linguistic intelligence ("word smart")

- Logical-mathematical intelligence ("number/reasoning smart")

- Spatial intelligence ("picture smart")

- Bodily-kinesthetic intelligence ("body smart")

- Musical intelligence ("music smart")

- Interpersonal intelligence ("people smart")

- Intrapersonal intelligence ("self smart")

- Naturalist intelligence ("nature smart")

Which intelligence suits the way the child best thinks and learns? Which one most engages the child in learning? Which one does the child need most to learn? As you observe and document, remember to keep the child's individual learning style in mind.

After the initial classroom entry, routinely observe the child in the context of daily activities, and watch how the child carries out activities while interacting with peers. Here's an example of the PLEASE C ME acronym in action.

Once while teaching kindergarten, I was influenced by a bright, small-framed, musically inclined kinesthetic learner named Jack. Jack had strong gross- and fine-motor skills and was socially accepted by his peers. His play was healthy, and he easily transitioned within the classroom setting. Jack was developmentally typical for his age. Then, after a two-week holiday break, Jack returned to class and roamed excessively. On his return, I started a new page of acronym loggings. Here are the "P" (physical) notes I recorded at that time:

> Since Jack's return from break, he continues to fiddle with his left ear. He has his finger wiggling in it chronically. Jack has also started roaming the classroom during free time. He hums loudly to himself.

Documenting Jack's behavior captured my attention, and the anecdotal loggings helped me easily root out the cause. A phone call to Jack's mother revealed that over the holiday break his eardrum was slightly punctured when he was playing with a stethoscope. The classroom roaming and loud humming was soothing to Jack. Using this information, his parents and I proceeded with a plan to alleviate Jack's excessive roaming and tend to his new physical need.

The roaming play challenge was promptly and effectively met through an assortment of sensory-integrated strategies. Jack's favorite was using PVC piping to listen to his voice while he played. The school occupational therapist made a head strap that specifically fit the hardware piping and Jack's head. This constant acoustic noise soothed him, especially during noisy periods of afternoon play. This strategy may not have worked on another child under the same circumstances.

Sensory Integration

Children learn when they use their senses during play. Sensory integration—the organization of sensations for use—allows controlled sensory input, which influences a child's learning potential and response to the environment. The seven senses of sensory integration—tactile, visual, auditory, olfactory, gustatory, proprioceptive, and vestibular—aligned with appropriate teaching strategies and techniques make way for desirable outcomes: increased adaptive behaviors, positive responses to motor issues, and graspable, creative connections to play. For example, while Sasha is digging a hole in her sandbox after a rainfall, she experiences sensations from the sand using her many senses:

- feeling the warm, gritty sand

- smelling wet sand

- recalling the weight of dry sand compared to the wet sand

- practicing motor skills

(Isbell and Isbell 2007, 19)

Sasha extends and deepens her play skills during the hands-on experience with sand. The activity emphasizes her learning potential and response to the environment largely because she is curious about and interested in it. She experiences the sand with all her senses and is actively and pleasantly engaged in the hands-on play.

The following three principles guide the use of sensory-integration techniques and strategies to address play challenges.

1. Sensory-integrated play should be uniquely tailored to an individual child using learning and playing steps based on PLEAS C ME notes. Position the child to succeed. When the child experiences success, play challenges can be redirected most effectively.

2. The child's distinct play preferences should be used in order to increase play potential and decrease play challenges. Then play challenges can be exchanged for new, useful play strategies in response to the sensory-integration exercises presented to the child.

3. Enriching and strengthening a child's play habits with sensory integration should stimulate the child's interests. When sensory-integration play activities are fun and engaging, the child will want to participate.

Children who are offered play experiences that are intentionally planned with the seven senses of sensory integration in mind are capable of not only overcoming play and learning difficulties but also pushing their abilities and exceeding expectations. Sensory-integrated play activities can tremendously increase a child's ability to navigate through the world. The child can become more attuned to details and processes versus final products when guided with stimulating sensory materials and activities of interest. Sensory integration productively increases self-confidence, intensely jump-starts learning, and extends and improves overall development and function.

Let's look closely at the seven senses of sensory integration.

1. **The tactile sense** (sense of touch). The tactile sense allows a child to navigate a world of pressure, temperature, and reaction to touch securely and comfortably. A child's tactile systems extend far beyond fingertips. Here are a few tactile-system sensations:

   - kissing a parent on the cheek
   - giving or receiving a big bear hug
   - being patted or massaged on the back
   - wearing fuzzy socks
   - playing in sand or water
   - feeling the temperature of a warm bath
   - falling and scraping a knee
   - getting rug burns
   - being tickled
   - using a toothbrush

2. **The visual sense** (sense of sight). A child's visual sense centers largely on what the child sees and how the child chooses to respond to it. A child's sight is closely connected to motor skills. Ask a child to hop, and watch as she instantly looks at her feet to make sure they are hopping correctly. Here are a few examples of the sense of sight:

   - attempting to catch a ball
   - reading a book
   - copying something from a chalkboard
   - noticing somebody's eye color
   - typing or handwriting a letter
   - stringing beads
   - putting together a puzzle
   - gazing at a breathtaking full moon

3. **The auditory sense** (sense of hearing). The auditory sense involves not only hearing a sound, but also *how* the sound is heard. We all respond differently to sound loudness, pitch, length, and location. Examples of the auditory sense are:

    - noticing obnoxious or serene background noise

    - hearing the vacuum cleaner *vroom* or the phone ring

    - listening to someone speak

    - attending an opera

    - interacting in a crowded room

    - paying attention to birds chirping, rain falling, or thunder raging

    - engaging in the Hokey Pokey

4. **The olfactory sense** (sense of smell) and 5. **the gustatory sense** (sense of taste). The senses of smell and taste are intensely interconnected. They technically work as one. Ponder this question: Have you ever been punished by a stuffy nose on Thanksgiving Day through being unable to fully taste the food? Pumpkin pie just doesn't go down the same—a real taste bud bummer! Here are a few examples of the amazing senses of smell and taste teamwork:

    - smelling fresh, out-of-the-oven cookies and having your mouth water

    - distinguishing between distinct food textures, tastes, and aromas

    - smelling a lemon and puckering your mouth

    - holding your nose and being unable to taste a food

6. **The proprioceptive sense** (sense of body position). A child's world is one multisensory sensation after another. The proprioceptive sense is a major sensory receptor, telling a child where his body parts are without having to look at them while maneuvering throughout a busy world (Biel and Peske 2005, 33). Examples of the proprioceptive sense include:

    - wrestling

    - sweeping or vacuuming the floor

    - doing push-ups

    - walking like a crab

- throwing balls

- wiping tables

- swimming

- pulling a wagon full of heavy objects

7. **The vestibular sense** (sense of balance and movement). The vestibular sense can be explained by two childhood favorites—swinging and spinning. Remember all the play provided by tire swings and playground swings, hammocks, scooters, and swiveling office chairs? Remember swinging forward and backward, sitting upright but also lying tummy down, or winding up the swing—twisting it as tight as you could—and then letting go? Here are additional examples of the vestibular sense:

   - jumping rope or jumping on a minitrampoline

   - riding in a wagon

   - rocking in a chair

   - marching

   - tumbling

   - riding a teeter-totter

   - riding a scooter board on your tummy

As you use the seven senses of sensory integration to individualize student play activities, remember it is pertinent to build on a child's sensory strengths to help overcome play challenges. Additionally, keep in mind that although children develop sensory skills and developmental skills at varying speeds, they need to master the coordination of "*all* seven senses to learn about their world and function effectively" (Isbell and Isbell 2007, 14).

The Use of Sensory Integration for Play Challenges

A majority of licensed occupational therapists use child-directed, sensory-integrated play activities to treat children with developmental play challenges. Many use them for children with debilitating deficits in the organization of their senses and for children who suffer from under- or overstimulation of their seven senses—senses that encourage, enhance, and stimulate healthy play as well as growth and development.

One such licensed therapist is Lilly Davis. I latched on to Ms. Lilly while working as a multi-impaired special educator on a native Indian reservation in New Mexico. Ms. Lilly worked alongside my students and me for a number of years using child-directed sensory integration and became a sounding board for the sensory-integration play techniques and strategies practiced by me and many other educators. She has thirty years of experience as an occupational therapist, and to this day, Ms. Lilly and I work well together because we both consider the following points about sensory integration important and beneficial to children who are struggling with play challenges:

1. Sensory integration combined with play effectively integrates a child's seven senses and enhances development.

2. Making sensory-integrated play exercises successful is largely a matter of approach.

3. A sensory-integration diet, otherwise known as a sensory diet, is often beneficial for children experiencing play challenges.

4. It is the responsibility of early care and education professionals to make sensory-integrated activities accessible as well as developmentally and age appropriate.

5. Sensory-integration play activities, practices, and materials should be adapted as necessary for children with special needs.

6. A child should not be pressured to participate in sensory-integrated activities.

7. Children who contend with play challenges should not be labeled as such, especially during play activities or in front of peers.

8. Children need to be held responsible for assisting in sensory-integration play cleanup, regardless of how messy.

9. Play challenges should be addressed in inspiring, healthy, and extraordinary ways, consistently using an organized sensory-integrated play schedule of sensory-integrated play activities and exercises, guidance, and patience.

Sensory integration combined with play effectively integrates a child's seven senses and enhances development. It does this by naturally improving gross- and fine-motor skills, increasing self-confidence, lengthening attention span, and building social skills.

Making sensory-integrated play exercises successful is largely a matter of approach. Sensory-integrated play exercises can be effective when you plug in directly to a child's unique formula for learning and unique ways of avoiding learning situations or everyday scenarios that are difficult. Try to understand the child's viewpoint by considering his or her attempts to cope with or manipulate through the frustration of an uncomfortable learning task. The combination of the tactile, vestibular, and proprioceptive senses is strongly recommended by a majority of occupational therapists. For children experiencing play challenges, this triad approach often produces the most progress in the shortest amount of time. When combined appropriately, these three senses work significantly well together. For more information on this approach, check out the following resources:

Sensational Kids: Hope and Help for Children with Sensory Processing Disorder (SPD) by Lucy Jane Miller

The Everything Parent's Guide to Sensory Integration Disorder: Get the Right Diagnosis, Understand Treatments, and Advocate for Your Child by Terri Mauro

A sensory-integration diet, otherwise known as a sensory diet, is often beneficial for children experiencing play challenges. The sensory diet, a term popularized by occupational therapist Patricia Wilbarger, is a personalized activity and play schedule that provides throughout the day select sensory input for a particular child. Children have different needs and personal profiles; therefore, sensory diets should be individually prepared for children. Most occupational therapists who are well trained in sensory integration are capable of preparing an individualized sensory diet. Although parental involvement is vital to a child's overcoming play challenges with the use of sensory-integration play exercises, parents should not attempt to construct a sensory diet without the professional guidance of a trained occupational therapist. Teachers and parents should work closely with a trained occupational therapist to implement and guide a child's individual sensory diet. For more information on sensory diets, check out these resources:

The Out-of-Sync Child: Recognizing and Coping with Sensory Integration Dysfunction by Carol Stock Kranowitz

Sensory Integration and the Child: Understanding Hidden Sensory Challenges by A. Jean Ayres

Sensory Integration: A Guide for Preschool Teachers by Christy Isbell and Rebecca Isbell

It is the responsibility of early care and education professionals to make sensory-integrated activities accessible as well as developmentally and age appropriate. Let's break that statement down:

- Accessible: Allow the child to access and use in a proper and safe manner equipment, supplies, and activities, regardless of the child's ability or special need.

- Developmentally appropriate: Ensure sound teaching practices are based on observation, responsiveness, and the development of each child as an individual and unique learner.

- Age appropriate: Provide activities and materials that are developmentally appropriate and safe for the child's age level.

Sensory-integration play activities, practices, and materials should be adapted as necessary for children with special needs. Use the following questions as a guide. Does the adaptation increase the child's ability to play and to function within play independently? Does the adaptation foster the child's interactions with peers and the environment? Does the adaptation aid in the development of the child's play skills? Does the adaptation promote cooperative play? Does the adaptation still allow the child to be positively challenged? Does the adaptation uphold developmentally appropriate practices?

A child should not be pressured to participate in sensory-integrated activities. Pressuring a child to participate in an activity will usually do more harm than good and slow the process of addressing play challenge issues. Children develop at an individual pace. The use of sensory-integrated play experiences stimulates a child's personal pace and activates a more intense learning direction.

Children who contend with play challenges should not be labeled as such, especially during play activities or in front of peers. Unfortunately, many children grow to feel inept, untalented, and frustrated due to early childhood labels. Children often outgrow awkward stages and challenges with age or with effective early intervention for play challenges.

Children need to be held responsible for assisting in sensory-integration play cleanup, regardless of how messy. Cleanup is an important part of the play process that is often left out. By working and cleaning up together in a group or as a pair, children learn to appreciate not only each other's help and abilities, but also one another's way of doing things. Responsibility is also instilled during cleanup. Children will feel as though they are making a difference.

Address play challenges in inspiring, healthy, and extraordinary ways, consistently using an organized sensory-integrated play schedule of sensory-integrated play activities and exercises, guidance, and patience. Intervening in a play challenge with the use of sensory-integrated activities isn't an overnight procedure. Implementation of intervention strategies is well worth the time and effort it takes for the child and for you!

The following chapters are organized according to five individual play challenges: dabbling, roaming, anxious, detached, and rejected. Extraordinary sensory-integration play ideas, exercises, and activities for children grappling with each of these play challenges inundate each chapter. Sensory-integration play tips within the chapters are referred to as Ms. Lilly SI Play Tips. Without Ms. Lilly's three decades of experience as an occupational therapist using sensory integration, the play tips wouldn't be what you'll quickly discover they are: *extraordinary!* You'll also discover bits of wisdom from Ms. Lilly, referred to as Ms. Lilly SI Points to Ponder.

I highly recommend that you read the following books in conjunction with this one:

So This Is Normal Too?: Teachers and Parents Working Out Developmental Issues in Young Children by Deborah Hewitt

Play: The Pathway from Theory to Practice by Sandra Heidemann and Deborah Hewitt

Practical Solutions to Practically Every Problem: The Early Childhood Teacher's Manual by Steffen Saifer

Each chapter contains a description of the play challenge, reasons for it, key intervention guidelines, and sensory-integration strategies to prompt play. Many of the play challenge strategies can be used to address multiple play challenges. A strategy in chapter 4, "Securing the Anxious Child to Play," for example, may also be used for a child who is experiencing a detached play challenge, which is discussed in chapter 5, "Connecting the Detached Child to Play." As a professional educator, you can modify the intervention strategies according to your needs.

Each chapter also contains a practical individual play plan that illustrates how a particular play challenge could be addressed. An individual play plan resembles a basic IEP, or Individualized Education Program, but is intended to help target play challenges affecting a child's involvement and progress in the general curriculum or, for preschoolers (and younger children), participation in appropriate play activities. An individual play plan can guide your work to include, support, and review the child's strengths, needs, and other observable and measurable performance data in the areas of play that affect learning.

Appendix A contains a list of common early childhood social and emotional developmental milestones to be achieved by a somewhat older child. When questions regarding play challenges arise, refer to this list to inform your perspective regarding typical development. A blank individual play plan can be found in appendix B. Appendix C is a list of creative things to use with an individual play plan and with sensory-integration play strategies. Appendix D contains a sample parent questionnaire.

Please note that an individual play plan and other strategies provided in this book are not replacements for an assessment or treatment plan by a medical professional. If a play challenge persists, seek an outside professional opinion.

Use of all suggested online sensory games, supplies, furniture, utensils, and activities is at your discretion. Please consider age appropriateness and safety for the children in your care. Also, as URLs change often, I cannot guarantee that a Web site suggested in this book will still exist when you try to visit it.

Promoting Positive and Productive Play

Before diving in to the rest of *Come and Play*, review the following notions promoting positive play patterns for children. They naturally alleviate play challenges and will assist you overall while you wade through the extraordinary sensory-integration activities.

1. Make it a point to offer all children a diverse play menu inclusive of the following:

   - Constructive play: Play that involves making *things* from a variety of *things*. (Appendix C lists lots of *things*.)

- Outdoor play: Play engrossed in the outdoors and catering to exploratory interactions with nature and its elements of sunshine, dirt, rain, and bugs.

- Physical play: Play encompassing exercise and the use of gross-motor skills, such as running, hopping, skipping, and galloping.

- Cooperative play: Play stimulating social interaction with peers. Playdates are meaningful and advantageous for regular cooperative play.

2. Remember that many children naturally prefer one form of play to another. Individuality, personality, and distinct quirks will direct children's play choices.

3. Encourage and help children to gain healthy play habits by regularly playing with them. This may require an occasional game of catch or a tea party for two . . . with *you*! Be playful while modeling appropriate social interaction during play.

4. Suggest to parents that they monitor their child's use of media. Unfortunately, too many children today are robbed of valuable playtime and relational growth by limitless and unsupervised television, computer, or video game access.

5. Don't accept that "It was *just* a donut for breakfast. It was *just* a couple of cookies at lunch. It was *just* a large soda with dinner." No. It was *just* poor nutrition! Proper nutrition in a child's life is vital. It can make or break natural energy levels and behavior for productive play patterns. Direct parents to complete nutritional guidelines for children via the following online resources:

- www.keepkidshealthy.com

- www.eatright.org

- www.nutrition.gov

6. Remember that fatigue is a play thief. Proper rest is a key component to keeping children healthy and alert for productive playtime. Offer in a newsletter to parents practical sleep suggestions for children. Check out *Healthy Sleep Habits, Happy Child* by Marc Weissbluth to review the basics.

7. Set up an inviting play environment. A child's play area should safely holler, "Come and play!" Avoid piled-high toys, sharp table corners and objects, and access to cabinets with toxic

products. Play areas shouldn't be cluttered, overstimulating, or understimulating.

8. Reward positive playtime with or without peers. Children are self-centered creations by nature. Learning to share and play nicely is a continual work in progress. When you see a child has made great strides in this area, be complimentary. Praise the child, and when appropriate, tangibly reward the behavior.

9. Incorporate positive play rituals. Set aside time each day for children to play. If the sun is shining, go outside to play! Model the precedence of play. Two great examples of play rituals to share with parents are:

    • Pump up the play volume of a summer birthday celebration by incorporating a kickball game at a park. After the ball game, slice and serve a huge watermelon—after washing everyone's hands, of course. Have the children pick out all the slippery seeds.

    • For a winter celebration, go bowling. Serve popcorn and other light snacks to satisfy any cravings for munchies while working the lanes.

10. To effectively promote positive play, grasp the power of it. The use of consistent, sensory-integrated play activities in a child's life can be developmentally monumental. Internationally renowned child psychologist David Elkind expresses in his book *The Power of Play: How Spontaneous, Imaginative Activities Lead to Happier, Healthier Children*, "Play is not a luxury but rather a crucial dynamic of healthy physical, intellectual, and social-emotional development at all age levels" (2007, 4). Play is what gets kids ready for learning in the first place.

Now, let's get busy helping children overcome play challenges by showing them how to creatively play in extraordinary sensory-integrated ways!

*Little by little
does the trick.*

—Aesop

Prompting the Dabbling Child to Play

What does it mean to dabble? *Merriam-Webster's Collegiate Dictionary* says it is "to work or involve oneself superficially or intermittently." All children dabble in play every now and then. Excessive dabbling, however, does not support a child's overall growth and development and can cause problems for later learning if intervention is not early. Children who consistently dabble in play are not investing in and building critical foundational skills for becoming successful learners and exploratory players. This chapter focuses on children who struggle with continual dabbling during playtime. These children resemble dabbling Mia in the example that follows.

Dabbling Mia

Mia's kindergarten teacher, Ms. Furner, set up an exploratory soil center in the classroom. She put down a large tarp and filled four large paint buckets with wet potting soil and hidden treasures, such as earthworms, seeds, and other toss-ins. Next to the big buckets Ms. Furner placed shovels, cups, spoons, funnels, and small cars. The children enjoy the center immensely!

One day Emmitt and Mia enter the play center. Emmitt immediately and eagerly begins plunging his hands into the wet soil and patting up mud balls. Mia displays little interest in the activity. She simply holds a small shovel and repeatedly dips it into one of the buckets. Emmitt explores the mud with intensity and intrigue while Mia aimlessly looks around without regard to the other children or materials. Emmitt's approach to the mud center is one of enthusiasm and wonderment. He's loving it! Mia's attitude toward the mud play is wooden and lifeless. If Mia's unmotivated and unfocused behavior consistently persists in other play centers or content areas over time, she could be experiencing a dabbling play challenge.

A child may be demonstrating a dabbling play challenge if the following behaviors persist in a consistent pattern over an extended period of time:

- The child plays irregularly and without active engagement.

- The child plays with little or no intrinsic motivation.

- The child fails or refuses to attempt anything new in play.

- The child engages in continually unconnected repetitive play motions, such as aimlessly poking at playdough or pointlessly stroking a paintbrush up and down.

- The child displays unfocused perseverative actions, repetitive actions a child gets stuck on (Biel and Peske 2005, 64). Examples include continually "scissoring" the air or flying a "finger" airplane during playtime.

- The child appears noticeably indifferent to play activities and materials.

- The child appears unaware of how to initiate or enter play with peers.

Reasons a Child May Dabble

A child may dabble in play for a variety of reasons.

- A child may dabble in play because of immaturity, regression, or delayed developmental skills. Consider a child's play like a flower. Play should sprout and then bloom and bloom and bloom! Taking into consideration that all children arrive at development milestones at their own pace, chronically stagnant or immature play is not developing play. Immature play is play that is obviously below the child's age level or below that of same-age peers. The play is overly silly or too aggressive. Regressive or delayed play-stage development is not blooming play either. For example, a four-year-old child who bangs blocks week after week while his peers engage in experimental, imaginative, and progressive block play (building exuberant block towers and incorporating knights and dragons, for example) is waving a developmental red flag. Because children develop differently, it is important to journal about a child's persistent developmentally inappropriate behaviors to supply leverage if a formal evaluation is needed.

- A child may dabble in play because she is unable or unaware how to gain entry into a playgroup or situation. Acquiring play negotiation and entry skills requires experience and confidence. The lack of these could be caused by poor social or verbal skills. A child who is experiencing difficulty gaining entry into play may linger on the outskirts of it, tossing out wishful verbal suggestions, such as, "When I play blocks at home, I always save the big ones for the bottom of my tower. I can show you how I do it." Dabblers who struggle in this area require assistance in developing self-confidence and acquiring appropriate prosocial skills as well as skills that encourage self-direction.

- A child may dabble in play because intrinsic motivation is not present. Intrinsic motivation, motivation from within, is a major factor in a child's play. As with adults, different things motivate different children. Dinosaurs may spark hearty play for one child but not for another. Another child may enjoy castles of all shapes and sizes. Making sure activities are age appropriate and individually appealing is extremely important for encouraging intrinsic motivation. A child should lose himself in play. This is difficult if the activity is too easy, too hard, or not stimulating. Children who are persistently not motivated from within to explore and discover in play may require direct adult intervention in the form of specific play-tutoring strategies. Play tutoring is when a teacher models and directs a child's play while providing reinforcement for his effort and ideas (Van Hoorn et al. 2003, 101). This kind of strategy "increases the instances and quality of a child's sociodramatic play and improves cognitive performance" (Ward 1996, 20). For guidance on how to conduct play-tutoring strategies, refer to *Play at the Center of the Curriculum* by Judith Van Hoorn, Patricia Monighan Nourot, Barbara Scales, and Keith Rodriquez Alward.

- A child may dabble in play because of passive personality traits. A child's personality evolves as she attempts to satisfy physical and emotional needs while carrying out everyday activities, such as playing and interacting with classmates (Van Hoorn et al. 2003, 309). Children with passive personalities are often inactive and submissive in the process of developing healthy play habits. A passive child may stare for long periods of time before communicating a need or want. A passive child may be shy, sensitive, or have poor eye contact with peers and teachers. The passive child also tends to be a spectator. A passive child may resemble one, for example, who during playtime is easily coaxed into handing over favorite classroom toys for those that are less appealing. Her playmates easily manipulate the items away from her, and she doesn't voice disapproval but only watches playmates play with "her" toy.

- A child may dabble in play because of poor motor planning. Motor planning is the ability to do physical things in sequence, such as holding both feet together while jumping and landing with both feet together (Biel and Peske 2005, 22). Dabblers with poor motor planning can become easily frustrated when their ability to motor plan breaks down. They often give up in play when an obstacle presents itself. For example, a child might attempt to climb an outdoor hanging rope ladder and understand how to progress up the ladder, but his hands and feet don't cooperate in sequence to advance upward. Think about it this way: Can you pat your head and rub your belly at the same time?

- A child may dabble in play because she is stuck in play. A child may dabble in play simply because she doesn't know where else to go with the play materials or activities. According to theorists, play has distinguishable features. A child may need assistance in becoming "unstuck" if the following points are observed in her play:

1. The child has exhausted all known play activity possibilities and intrinsic motivation has vanished.

2. The child is no longer actively engaged in the play activity.

3. The child suddenly is more focused on attending to the end of the play activity rather than the means of it.

4. The child's once playful, nonliteral behavior has turned rigid and pressing.

5. The child's play is restrained, not free.

(Van Hoorn et al. 2003, 5)

Key Intervention Guidelines

To prompt the dabbling child to play, use creative thinking, nature, and music activities along with the seven senses of sensory integration. When prompting play, model progression through the play activity, preferably in guided steps or a sequencing of skills. Be sensitive to and respectful of the child who may not want you in his play space. Play intervention works only when the child is receptive. Barging in and forcing a child to "do this" or to "do that" doesn't support positive play efforts. A fine line exists between letting a child "play out" problems for a while and intervening before the problem flourishes. Remember that journaling is especially helpful, as is looking closely at a child's individual PLEAS C ME information. Journal in detailed notes about when and how intensely children dabble. Doing so will help you discover patterns or uncover root causes.

Key intervention strategies for prompting a dabbling child to play are:

- Enhance the curriculum and play materials regularly and creatively.

- Change the environment and rotate play materials regularly and creatively.

- Connect dabblers to a play-directing peer (a play buddy). Pair the child with a zealous playtime peer. Peer modeling is wonderful for dabbling children.

- Keep the atmosphere noncompetitive and orderly.

- Lock directly into the dabbling child's personal interests and learning style.

The coming pages present extraordinary ideas and activities to jump-start a dabbling child toward, in, or through play, and activities are listed for each intervention strategy listed above. Keep the following objectives in mind while wading through the ideas.

1. Clearly look at the definition of a dabbling play challenge and at intervention strategies for a child's dabbling behavior. Sometimes the answer to dabbling is as plain as the nose on your face. Before identifying a child as having a dabbling play challenge, make sure the child

   - is simply not paying attention to what she's doing;

   - is not disinterested in the offered play materials because she needs the materials tweaked to peak her interest;

   - is not tired, bored, or unwell;

   - has not exhausted all possibilities for play center items or materials and is needing the activity to be enhanced.

2. Be sure to review the key intervention strategies for a dabbling child that begin on page 29 while keeping in mind the three principles of sensory integration on page 13. It is important to frequently revisit the three principles of sensory integration to reestablish the purpose of positioning a child to succeed within sensory-rich activities that are pleasurable and that shout, "Come and play!"

3. Rule out any basic health, vision, hearing, or learning disability possibilities that could be causing a dabbling play challenge.

4. If the dabbling persists or increases in intensity over time (after several documented intervention attempts), hold a conference with the child's parent or guardian. Consultation with an outside community resource may also be needed. Remember, early intervention is key!

5. As with all classroom, home, or center learning experiences, put safety, health, and age appropriateness at the forefront of all sensory-integration play exercises. Always keep activities individualized, nonthreatening, and unforced.

Sensory-Integration Strategies to Prompt a Dabbling Child to Play

The coming pages provide a backdrop for ideas and exercises to prompt a dabbling child to play. The activities are creative, novel, and hands on and can be simplified or extended for each child's needs and interests. Children will successfully respond to the strategies if fun remains at the forefront.

Use Creative Thinking Strategies to Prompt Play

Wonder is an important motivator for lifelong learning (Wilson 1997). Wonder-filled play endeavors for children should focus on process, not an end product. Sometimes a dabbling child may simply need a boost or a subtle prompt to get imaginative juices flowing. Try the following activities to imaginatively prompt a dabbling child to play.

LET'S THINK TOGETHER: With the child who dabbles, sit facing each other in two deep beanbags, preferably touching your feet to the child's, and engage the child with thought-provoking questions. Hand him a ball and ask, "What other things are round like a ball that we could play with together?" Use different colored objects, an assortment of Frisbees, textured beanbags, or interesting items from nature like a locust or snail shell to prompt questions, such as, "What do you think this snail did in his shell all day?" Musical instruments or interesting tools like a tuning fork are resourceful thought provokers. You can ask, "Why do you think this fork vibrates the way it does when struck?"

WHAT IF: Have the child who dabbles close her eyes. Hand her an imaginative prop, such as a stuffed play kitten, a set of butterfly wings from the dramatic play area, or a birthday hat. Ask prompting questions: "What if you found a kitten in your desk today? How would you play with it?" "What if you woke up tomorrow and could fly? Where is the first place you'd fly?" "What if your birthday was every day? Who would you invite to your party?"

Ms. Lilly
SI Point to Ponder

How would you describe a creative child? Over the years, I've observed that creative children tend to be imaginative, spontaneous, intuitive, persistent, and very curious. They thrive on asking, "Why?" As an educator or child care provider, do you consider yourself creative? The first step in nurturing a child's creativity is to reflect on your own.

Ms. Lilly
SI Play Tip

Use poetry and silly stories to encourage creative thinking for dabblers. Shel Silverstein penned the comical "What If?" and several other outrageously odd poems in his well-known book *Where the Sidewalk Ends.* Arlene Mosel wrote the fabulous *Tikki Tikki Tembo,* sure to spark laughter and imaginative thoughts. Children love racing to recite the tongue twisting "*Tikki tikki tembo-no sa rembo-chari bari ruchi-pip peri pembo!*"

Add hand or sock puppets and props to readings. Let a dabbler swing in a hammock during the reading. Play soft nature sounds in the background while reading and prompting the play.

ANOTHER WHAT IF: Preferably during circle time (this activity requires a large, open area), inform children, "We will be playing a pretend game called, 'What if our classroom was filled to the ceiling with _____?'" Fill in the blank with anything you wish—maybe it's mashed potatoes! Ask follow-up questions, such as, "Show me how you would move in a room full of mashed potatoes. How would your body feel covered in mashed potatoes? Would you eat any?" Get creative with "what if" possibilities. Provide children with hands-on "what if" props if possible. For example, giving a small bowl of mashed potatoes to each child while discussing the questions will enhance the activity. Here are a few "what if" favorites:

- What if our classroom was filled to the ceiling with ice cream?

- What if our classroom was filled to the ceiling with peanut butter?

- What if our classroom was filled to the ceiling with gelatin?

- What if our classroom was filled to the ceiling with thumbtacks?

- What if our classroom was filled to the ceiling with honey?

- What if our classroom was filled to the ceiling with moss?

- What if our classroom was filled to the ceiling with soda?

- What if our classroom was filled to the ceiling with toads?

FINISH THE LINE: Children who dabble often spout, "I don't know what to paint [or write or draw]. What do you think I should do?" To prompt the child forward in such activities, initiate and model the first step in a parallel sitting position (that is, you and the child sitting side by side). If drawing, for example, draw one line on the paper with something other than a pencil. Here's a list of writing utensils to use:

- scented marker: Crayola's include colors such as dragon drool red and belching baboon yellow. The zany smells are sure to tickle a child's funny bone and imagination.

- Crayola OverWriters: markers that color over each other

- ultra fine, chisel tip, or metallic marker

- weighted pen

- Twist 'n' Write pencil (www.coolsafetyproducts.com)

- Do-A-Dot marker or marker bottle

- vibrating pen; it's battery operated

- feather pen

- gel pen

- fat ballpoint pen

- dual-ended pen or marker

- chalk or chalk pencil (www.dickblick.com)

- finger or large triangular crayon (www.beyondplay.com)

Ms. Lilly
SI Play Tip

Marker bottles have a no-spill tip and are easy for small children to manipulate.

Finger crayons teach eye-hand coordination, motor control, counting, and colors. Every classroom should invest in a set or two.

Take note of the child's reaction to play possibilities with pens. Like adults, children can establish favorite writing utensils. To eliminate squabbling, keep duplicates of high-interest items.

When modeling play, make the line you're drawing squiggly, crooked, stair-stepped, jagged, or dotted. Explain that the two of you will take turns drawing. You draw the first line, and he will draw the second line. Continue together until the masterpiece is completed. Do the same with words when writing or a stroke of paint when painting. If the child finds himself in the same place the next day, initiate the start of the line as before, but phase yourself out earlier. Try to do as little as possible. You don't want to enable the play challenge.

The *Draw Write Now* series by Marie Hablitzel and Kim Stitzer is an excellent resource series for dabbling children who struggle with creativity in writing or drawing activities.

ANIMAL CHARADES: Play a game of animal charades with a child who dabbles. You may want to include a few other children or the whole class. Pretend to be domesticated animals, such as dogs, snakes, or cats, making only motions, not noises. Or act out wild animals like alligators, giraffes, anteaters, or raccoons. This game is not only engaging and fun but also allows children to stretch their imagination and muscles.

HOW ELSE: Gather a variety of everyday items, such as an oversized T-shirt, paper plate, magazine, ball, paper clip, and tablecloth. First, allow children to investigate the props hands on. Then encourage them to think of other ways to use the items. For example, the oversized T-shirt may be used as a baby blanket. Have children explain their answers aloud.

Use Nature to Prompt Play

Nature directly and positively complements a child's learning processes. A classroom simply cannot duplicate the firsthand observation and learning possibilities in nature—the fresh air and brilliant setting alone are unmatchable. In nature, "school" is literally anywhere! Exposing children who dabble to nature increases learning and playing potential through the seven senses, as well as provides intriguing experiences. Nature can "naturally" aid children who dabble in becoming securer and more independent and successful players. Try the following activities to prompt a dabbling child to play using nature. Additional nature activities can be found beginning on page 108.

FINDING SHAPES AND COLORS IN NATURE: Take a child who dabbles outside with an Etch A Sketch or Lite-Brite Travel (www.hasbro.com) and have her find a variety of shapes in nature. "Suzy, can you find something in the shape of a triangle? Can you point out something orange? Draw it on the Etch A Sketch, and I'll try to guess what it is!" Mini Etch A Sketch toys are available and less bulky.

Enhance the activity by hauling the child who dabbles with a peer (take class turns, of course) in a wagon around the playground to observe and "etch." Ask enhancing and discriminating questions regarding observed shapes, colors, textures, odors, and sizes in nature.

PETAL BLOWING: Gather a variety of artificial or natural flower petals. Pay attention to allergies when using natural flower petals. Put down a long piece of tape on one end of a classroom table. Have the child who dabbles stand at the other end of the table and try to blow the petals past the line of tape. Make it a two-child game, and see who can blow the most petals over the line.

To expand on the game, let the children use tweezers or chop sticks to pick up and sort the petal varieties in muffin tins or small cups. Feathers, cotton balls, or heavier items work as well as petals. Have the children blow through straws, plastic tubes, or noisy party blowers to push the petals along. Or toss in paint, letting children dip empty thread spools in paint and blow them around on paper in a tray with bendy straws.

Ms. Lilly
SI Play Tip

The Museum of Modern Art store at www.momastore.org has a fabulous selection of constructible drinking straws. Create awesome twisting and bending designs to fiddle, blow, or drink with!

BERRY BOUNCING: My grandmother taught me that fresh cranberries bounce! Bouncing them is how she would test them before making seasonal cranberry bread (which was heavenly). She would hold a cranberry above her head and drop it. If it bounced, we washed it, sliced it, and tossed it in the mixing bowl. If it didn't bounce, we "bounced" it into the trash can. Have a child who dabbles do the berry bounce. Put a twelve-inch piece of tape on the floor. Tape a small, six-inch square directly in front of the taped line. Have the child put his toes behind the line, and hand him a cranberry. Have him hold it directly in the air over the taped box and drop it, trying to hit inside the box. If the berry bounces, put it in a berry box. If not, put it in the trash can. Expand on the activity by making cranberry bread in class. The child who dabbles can add the cranberries and stir the batter.

A NATURE COLLECTION: For a simple sensory nature activity, take children on a nature walk. Give each child a brown paper bag for collecting outside items. Look for acorns, fallen bark chunks, pinecones and pine needles, and leaves of all shapes and sizes. Allow children sensory experiences, such as running their fingers over the top of a tree stump or feeling cold mud. Bring magnifying glasses, binoculars, sunglasses, kaleidoscopes, butterfly nets, and prisms to enhance the nature walk. Encourage children to listen for sounds, such as a bird chirping, the wind whooshing, a dog barking, or fall leaves crunching as you walk on them. After the nature walk, use the collected items to make a nature mobile with yarn and a hanger. A nature collage is another resourceful idea for collected nature walk items.

NATURE MATCHING: Take digital pictures of a variety of items in nature. Show children the pictures and have them identify each picture by matching it with something they've seen outside. Make some of the pictures easy to match, such as a recognizable tree the children pass by every day. Make others not so easy to match, such as a close-up shot of a blade of grass. This activity is versatile. Children can venture outdoors and match picture to picture, or during circle time verbally recall identification and location of the item after viewing the picture.

Ms. Lilly
SI Play Tip

Offer a variety of magnifying-glass tools for outside discovery and play. Try Magnifier Boxes for observing nature specimens and soil, Super Bug Viewers, which more than double the size of bugs and have built-in air holes, or Big See/Little See lenses, which have one side that enlarges size and the other that reduces size. Visit Nasco for these items and other teaching aids at www.eNasco.com.

PLANT BULBS, HERBS, OR VEGGIES: Let children get down and dirty! Help them plant a playground section of bulbs, herbs, or veggies. Safe bulb choices include daffodils, tulips, and crocuses. Children can plant an herb garden according to themes, such as a spaghetti garden (parsley, oregano, fennel, and basil), a teatime garden (chamomile, lemon, balm, spearmint, and peppermint), or a "scent"-sational garden (lilac, lemon, lavender, mint, rosemary, and thyme). Be creative with garden setup and décor.

GO ON A BUG HUNT: Take classmates on a hunt for bugs, snails, worms, and spiders. Observe the living creatures and discuss how certain bugs creep, crawl, or fly. Enhance the hunt by playing insect charades. Sing songs, such as "The Eensy Weensy Spider" or "Bringing Home a Baby Bumblebee."

Use Music to Prompt Play

Music naturally sets a child's play stage for more complex thinking. Combine sensory movement with music and you'll generate a more active, creative, and spontaneous play environment. Music helps children in the following ways:

- listen better

- advance language skills

- discriminate sounds

- explore their senses

- remember more

- transition from one activity to another with ease

- think critically

- develop social and cognitive skills

Music combined with the seven senses of sensory integration can significantly increase listening, learning, and play potential for children. Here are a few creative ways to prompt a child who dabbles to play using music.

HANDMADE BAND MUSIC: Make homemade instruments, such as the following, for an in-class marching band:

Ms. Lilly
SI Play Tip

Let children discover how earthworms dig without hands, hear without ears, see without eyes, smell without noses, and move without feet using Worm Vue Wonders, available online. Ant farms are awesome to observe too!

- guitars: use a tissue box with rubber bands strapped across the top

- spoons: use metal spoons of different sizes

- washboard: use corrugated cardboard, and strum it with a stick or spoon

- maracas: use plastic soda bottles with stones secured inside

- tambourines: use paper plates stapled together, with beans or rice inside

- drums: use oatmeal boxes, big butter tubs, coffee cans, empty paint cans, wooden or stainless steel bowls, or pots and pans

- cymbals: use two metal pot lids, kettle lids, or pie tins

- gongs: use toy mallets or wooden spoons to strike metal objects

- sand blocks: use wooden blocks with sandpaper securely glued to them for children to rub together

- shakers: use keys to jingle and jangle, or plastic jars, milk jugs, paper bags, or butter tubs filled with rice and the lids on tight

Ms. Lilly
SI Play Tip

Don't forget that children can make a variety of sounds with their bodies. They can whistle, hum, sing, snap, clap, stomp, slap thighs, slide hands back and forth, click tongues, blow raspberries, tap toes, click heels, or pop cheeks. Children can also use their bodies to hiss, gasp, or shush—gently or loudly.

March around the classroom to a variety of music with children. Vary speeds as you march—super slow, super fast, medium slow, very slow, or as fast as the children can go. Venture online for other creative musical props, such as movement scarves, lollipop drums, ankle and wrist bells, finger cymbals, jingle sticks, triangle and bell sets, castanets, tambourines, sand blocks, rainmakers, boomwhackers, ribbon sticks, and wands.

MUSICAL TIPTOE TAPE: Put on the floor colored mechanical or duct tape in a variety of designs, such as curvy, straight, zigzag, parallel lines, or closed shapes. On the "tiptoe tape" have the child who dabbles—barefoot, in fuzzy socks, or in shoes—do the following:

- roll along the tape on his feet from heel to toe and back again

- walk on tiptoes along the tape, as if on a tight rope

- hop along the tape

- snake crawl along the tape
- inch along the tape like a wiggly worm
- scooter board along the tape
- jump rope back and forth over the tape

Add upbeat music, and ask the child to snap his fingers while raising his knees one at a time while walking along the tape. Use adhesive contact paper for sensory walking activities by securing the paper to the floor, sticky side up. Let children walk on it in fuzzy socks. Make and secure belt bands (chenille strings strung with bells) to a child's wrists or ankles to enhance the sensory experience. Expand on the activity by laying down thick mats for tumbling instead of walking along the tape. Sprinkle a little perfume or vanilla scent on the mat to incorporate more sensory integration into the experience.

BIGFOOT PLAY: Have a child who dabbles put on galoshes, moon walker's shoes (www.southpawenterprises.com). Oversized shoes often help children improve balance, coordination, and body awareness. Have a child who dabbles stomp around to music on large, securely placed colored circles. Try playing jazz, reggae, or symphony music.

VACUUM NOISE: In a partitioned area, toss small-sized cereal all over the floor. Have a child who dabbles make number and letter shapes as she sucks up the cereal with a handheld vacuum cleaner.

SOUND PLAY: Have children close their eyes, blindfolding persistent peekers, and encourage them to listen to and guess what sound you're making. Sounds may include clapping your hands, snapping your fingers, yawning, stapling papers, closing a door, and dropping a book on the floor. Then let children take turns making the discovery sounds!

Enhance the Curriculum and Play Materials for a Dabbling Child

The play materials available to children greatly affect their play and their behavior in play. Using the curriculum to enhance simple classroom activities or learning center materials can intrinsically nudge a child who dabbles toward play. Spark an interest! Let's look at all the motivating possibilities for paper, scissors, rocks, and . . . aah, playdough. The following are examples of such enhancements. Carry these ideas across the curriculum for use with other play materials and activities.

PAPER

Paper choices for enhancing an activity are abundant. Rotate paper regularly for a child who dabbles. And keep in mind that paper can be braided, crimped, cut, chained, curled, folded, rolled, twisted, fringed, perforated, torn, slit, punched with a hole punch, and traced on. Paper options include the following:

- adding machine tape: perfect for torn, folded, taped, or glued paper chains

- Bare Books: blank paper educational products—books, puzzles, journals, game boards, and more (www.barebooks.com)

- butcher paper: tape it to a wall and paint, draw, or glue items on it

- calendars, catalogs: let the child who dabbles cut away with a variety of scissors

- carbon paper: great for tracing activities

- cardboard, including trays and tubes of all sizes: possibilities for cardboard play and projects are limitless; for example, set out a big box and hand the child who dabbles a few scented markers, blopens, or fingerpaints

- card stock: useful for sturdy and pliable projects, for folding or cutting

- coffee filters: use for a quick eyedropper painting exercise or a folding activity

- construction paper: colors galore and many options, such as confetti, glitter, or heavyweight textured types

- contact paper: the sticky side makes for great sensory projects

- envelopes: all sizes can be used for quick and simple puppets or for storing unfinished projects

- fingerpainting paper: a must for every early childhood program or classroom—children love the glossy look

- gift wrap: great for wrapping pretend play gifts or for cutting, gluing, and folding; lots of textured play possibilities

Ms. Lilly
SI Play Tip

Instead of offering a child who dabbles ordinary rectangular or square pieces of paper for play, challenge her with a large, precut piece of paper shaped like a diamond, triangle, oval, or trapezoid. Use textured paper varieties (sandpaper, shiny wallpaper) regularly as well. Doing so will likely expand creative thought.

- graph paper: ideal for science centers or patterning within the squares

- greeting cards: excellent for cutting and pasting, including musical greeting cards

- grocery bags: provide lots of puppet or costume possibilities because they come in many useful sizes

- index cards: a wide variety of options—colored, lined, blank, 3 x 5 and larger

- magazines: great for collages or mere ripping, tearing, and crumpling

- newspaper: tremendous for stuffing exercises—having a child quickly stuff a pillowcase or large box with newspaper—or for folding hats of all kinds

- origami paper: the lightweight sheets and activity of origami are excellent for honing fine-motor skills

- packing paper: best found in shoe boxes, it's great for twisting into animal shapes

- paper plates: perfect for puppets and homemade musical instruments

- paper towels: spray lightly with water and let children draw on them with scented markers

- picture story lined writing paper by Edupress (www .highsmith.com/edupress): perfect for handwriting and illustrating stories

- poster board: great for splatter painting or focused cutting to hone fine-motor skills

- sandpaper: terrific for cutting out sensory stencils for tracing; cut strips of different textures and have children play a matching texture game, or for a change of pace, have children draw or write on sandpaper with a variety of writing utensils.

- tissue paper: another fine stuffing product, or toss it in a dramatic play center for making "mummies" or flowers

- tracing and typing paper: useful for folding activities

- wallpaper or sample paint color cards: scraps and samples are useful in an art center, and most hardware stores accommodate educators

SCISSORS

Being able to use scissors properly is an important developmental skill. Make sure children, especially those who dabble, have good quality cutting utensils. Check regularly for dull scissors. For children who have special needs or poor motor coordination, use double-handled training scissors with four rubber-coated finger holes, which allows you to practice scissoring with the child and build the child's confidence until he is able to use a single pair of scissors on his own.

Hobby and craft stores are filled with scissors that will cut straight, jagged, squiggly, crooked, and other ways. Fiskars (www .fiskars.com) has several varieties, including total control, soft grip, spring action, dual-control training, easy grip, long loop, and animal imprints. Scissors don't necessarily have to cut paper. A great idea is to place a pair of scissors at the playdough center. Cutting playdough is entertaining, and it also strengthens a child's fine-motor skills. Let children practice scissor skills with playdough by cutting out geometric and angular shapes.

ROCKS

Rocks can generate a wide variety of activities that prompt a child who dabbles to play. Rock exploration is ideal for dabbling children because rocks vary in texture, mass, color, shape, and size. Rock activities can include a simple rock sorting exercise or painting large, coarse stones outdoors. Rock centers can meet sensory objectives. For example, when teaching kindergarteners, I set up a rock play center during letter *R* week, and the possibilities expanded daily. I was amazed at how my students took to the center as they did the following:

- sketched on rocks with colored chalk
- sorted the rocks by size, color, and texture
- polished rocks with sandpaper
- ground up small rocks to experience friction and feel heat
- grew a class crystal rock garden
- separated rocks with unusual markings or features
- ordered rocks from lightest to heaviest
- glued small gravel rocks into sculptures
- turned a rock into a pet

- sifted and panned "gold"—gold-painted rocks in large tubs of colored water

- made rock candy and loved watching the crystals form

- used rock salt to make ice cream in coffee cans

Ms. Lilly
SI Play Tip

When working with playdoughs, have children put on their smocks or old clothes, and "muscle" the substance—squeeze it, spread it, squish it, pull it apart, pound it, mold it, twist it, poke it, smush it, and roll it! For children with weak muscle tone, put out cold playdough or molding clay. It's much more difficult to manipulate.

Ms. Lilly
SI Play Tip

Don't forget to offer children who dabble interesting decorations and accessories for working with playdough material. Decorations can include toothpicks, pipe cleaners, nuts, bolts, buttons, sequins, shells, twigs, golf tees, or wooden craft sticks. Accessories can include rolling pins, cookie cutters, funnels, melon scoopers, pastry tubes, plastic knives, pizza cutters, potato mashers, dough extruders, and proper storage containers. Children who dabble benefit from such curriculum and material enhancement.

PLAYDOUGHS, PAINTS, AND PASTES

Mixing up playdough, paints, pastes, and clay sensory-integration style for children who dabble is easy! The following fabulous sensory play substances are sure to entice a child who dabbles to play. Model proper playdough, paint, and paste play with the children, and discuss why the mixtures should not be eaten.

MUD MUCK: 2 cups mud, 2 cups sand, ¼ cup rice, ½ cup salt, 1 tsp. flavored extract

Slowly add ingredients together until the mixture is a desired consistency. Add cornstarch to thicken if needed.

SAWDUST STUFF: 2 cups laundry detergent, 2 cups sawdust, water, food coloring

Slowly add ingredients together until the mixture is a desired consistency and hue. Add cornstarch to thicken if needed.

GUNK: 2 cups salt, ½ cup oatmeal, ½ cup cornstarch, water

Mix salt and ⅔ cup water. Heat on stovetop at a low temperature for three to four minutes. Remove and add oatmeal, cornstarch, and ½ cup water. Stir vigorously. To achieve desired consistency, add more cornstarch to thicken or more water to thin.

OOEY STEW: 1 cup cornstarch, ¼ cup water, 2 drops food coloring, and desired number of toss-ins

Mix ingredients in a large mixing bowl to a stewlike consistency. Use cornstarch to control the texture. Change the texture of the mixture, making it extra sticky one day and more pourable the next. Add toss-ins, such as yarn scraps, crumbled dried flowers, lace bits, or colored salt and sand. Add bowls, cups, spoons, ladles, and measuring utensils for proper play.

SIMPLE SILLY SLIME: 1 cup white glue and 1 cup liquid starch (Sta-Flo)

Mix together one cup of each ingredient in a large bowl. Using a sturdy spoon, mix well. It takes some time to prepare the correct texture for this substance. As you mix, if the slime is too sticky, add starch. If it's too soupy, add more glue. The secret to this simple slime is keeping the two ingredients in balanced portions.

COFFEE GROUNDS: Several cups coffee grounds (wet or dry) and rice or grits (Amount needed will vary according to number of students—½ cup per student is desirable.)

Used coffee grounds (wet or dry) mixed with rice or grits is an awesome sensory play substance. Let a child who dabbles play with the mixture on wax paper or in a shallow tub with scoops and cups.

MASHED POTATOES: Leftover mashed potatoes can be easily turned into a usable play substance for dabbling children to manipulate on wax paper or a cookie sheet. Add water to thin out the spuds or wheat germ to thicken. The objective is to make the potatoes as stimulating to the hands and eyes as possible. Add coconut, frozen raisins, frozen peas, or sunflower seeds. Inedible additions work wonderfully too. Try small beads, colored sand, or small chunks of squishy Styrofoam. Remind children not to put things in their mouths.

Scented extracts, seasonings, and toss-ins and natural materials add sensory value to playdoughs, paints, and pastes. Consider using:

- scented extracts: lemon, almond, butter, maple, coconut, butterscotch, and orange extract, as well as the especially stimulating scents of vanilla (a calming scent), mint, and peppermint (two alerting scents)

- seasonings: nutmeg, pumpkin spice, cloves, cinnamon, basil, sage, oregano, and parsley

- toss-ins and natural materials: aquarium gravel, shiny pebbles, confetti, dried evergreen needles, cleaned and crushed egg shells, dried leaves and flowers, acorns, blades of grass, sequins, food coloring, rice, salt, glitter, sand, coffee grounds (wet or dry), oatmeal, cornmeal, sawdust, and seeds

Ms. Lilly
SI Play Tip

Here are a few texture tips and tidbits. Adding glitter to paint and pastes makes them shiny. Adding salt or sand makes them gritty. Adding sugar makes them sparkle when dry. Adding oil makes a slimy texture. Sand or cornstarch makes paint and paste thick and chunky. Rotate and vary textures, such as smooth and creamy, soft and pliable, wet and sticky, pebbled and lumpy, gritty and coarse, rubbery and slippery. The following list of describing words is to help children become familiar not only with texture but also with its meaning. For example, a child will not understand "velvety" unless she feels something velvety. The added bonus? The words will also expand a child's vocabulary.

bubbly	crumby	hairy	soupy
bumpy	furry	lumpy	stringy
chunky	fuzzy	prickly	waxy
clumpy	grainy	rubbery	wiry
crinkly	gritty	slimy	wooly

Change the Environment and Rotate Play Materials Regularly and Creatively

A classroom or child care environment should evolve, progress, and change as the year unfolds. Children who dabble require the rotation of play materials and the environmental setting to continually captivate their interest and stimulate play. Regularly changing a classroom setting and play materials doesn't require a lot of extra planning and effort. Keep in mind that changing a classroom environment can be accomplished in small, subtle ways. Put center or play materials away for a while, then bring them back after a few weeks and they'll be new again to children. Continue to add enticing, hands-on, open-ended materials of interest to centers. Here are other suggestions for rotating play materials and changing the environment:

- Change the room setup: Desks and tables can be put in groups to promote social interaction. Place them in rows to emphasize more independent work. A U-shaped desk or table arrangement is another idea. Change the room setup often, but make sure everyone can move around easily. The classroom shouldn't look or feel cramped.

- Use themes: Use seasonal or unit themes for decoration inspiration. Introduce plants and animals (class pets) into class routines and responsibilities.

- Combine centers: Combine learning centers for additional space and variety. For example, connect the craft center to the science center to make pinecone or leaf art.

- Post student work: Frame, display, and change student work regularly. Use creative and inventive methods. Remove outdated work. Rotate displays and classroom print pieces.

- Add music: Music has the potential to instantly change the mood, tone, focusing potential, and comfort level of a classroom. Rotate genres.

Connect Children Who Dabble to a Play-Directing Peer

Children learn a tremendous amount from one another. Less social children can become more social through regular interactions. When children take on a teacherlike role with their peers, cognitive and social development is significantly promoted. Some children instantly rise to the occasion, while others need time. When combined, the two personalities can fine-tune one another. The perfect chum combination—a naturally zealous player paired with a child who dabbles—can make all the difference in play direction and duration, ultimately catapulting play opportunities for the child who dabbles. When appropriately connected with a play buddy, children who dabble can practice at productively modeling play, stimulating social skills, negotiating frustration, and redirecting dabbling behaviors. A child who dabbles shouldn't be paired with a play buddy who is overpowering, bossy, or likely to take over the entire task. Aim for play buddy connections that are gentle as well as effective.

Several sensory-integration play activities targeted to play buddies follow. The activities naturally encourage conversation and peer participation with a pair of children of which one is a dabbler. Partition off the play area for more socio-dramatic play between the two children. Monitor, of course.

HAMBURGER MAKING: Set up a table with two big buckets filled with textured mud. Make it thick and chunky for extra muscle work! Rest a plank of wood across the two buckets. Tell the two children they will be making hamburgers and they must work together to make patties and place them on the wood. Demonstrate the process. Enhance the activity by providing tools, such as plastic spatulas, handheld mixers, and pepper grinders and saltshakers filled with extra-fine sand for "seasoning." Have the children wear kitchen gloves if desired. Use whatever else you can think of for making the hamburgers. Here are a few suggestions:

- Buns: Cut out bread shapes from sturdy cardboard or Styrofoam, or let children make buns from playdough.

- Toppings: Use Styrofoam packing squiggles as pickles, alpha sprouts as play onions, or precut fabric or foam as cheese. Be creative. The end goal is for the two children to act as a smooth-running and conversing hamburger-making machine.

Also try making spaghetti (thick yarn) with mud balls.

Ms. Lilly
SI Play Tip

Vary mud's texture. Make it thick by adding cornstarch, make it clumpy by adding petroleum gel, or make it gritty by adding sand. Children like to play in mud soup—thin mud mixed with a variety of natural toss-ins, scents, and such.

Ms. Lilly
SI Play Tip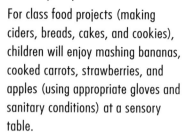

For class food projects (making ciders, breads, cakes, and cookies), children will enjoy mashing bananas, cooked carrots, strawberries, and apples (using appropriate gloves and sanitary conditions) at a sensory table.

Ms. Lilly
SI Play Tip

A sensory table can become a patchwork of scrap fabric possibilities, including burlap bits, carpet chunks, corduroy, cotton balls, denim, fur, gauze, netting, silk, terry cloth, velvet, vinyl, and wool. Sprinkle scents and toss-ins for variety.

SENSORY TABLE PLAYING: A sensory table is basically any clean container (box, trough, or tub, for example) filled with a tactile medium. The use of sensory tables is a developmentally appropriate practice for young children and caters wonderfully to social interaction among peers. Fine-motor skills can be honed in creative ways, too, with the use of a sensory table, but close supervision is required. Use a wading pool, baby bathtub, or traditional classroom water/sand table (adjustable height and see-through table options are available). Dampen table items for flare. Rotate the contents frequently, and remember to always consider the age appropriateness of the materials used. Possibilities for materials to use in an indoor or outdoor sensory table follow:

- aquarium gravel, pebbles, and stones in lots of colors
- buttons, beads, birdseed, and beans
- cornmeal, oatmeal, confetti, and crayon shavings
- dirt—soft, clods, or mud
- flower petals mixed with leaves, small pinecones, feathers, and other nature specimens
- fabric scraps
- flour or powdered milk with a variety of funnels, whisks, and beaters
- marbles and manipulatives (counters)
- pasta and noodles—cooked and uncooked
- poker chips of all different colors and sizes
- popcorn—popped or kernels
- rice—try buckets of colored rice
- sand—colored or natural, wet or dry
- shaving cream and shredded paper
- seashells of different shapes, colors, and sizes
- sponges, wet or dry, of all shapes and sizes
- Styrofoam pieces, packing peanuts, and pom-poms
- water tinted with food coloring, scents, or extracts and Silly String, ice cubes, or other toss-ins
- wiggly craft eyes—available in multipacks, featuring a variety of sizes and colors

Add toys to a sensory table, such as small dinosaurs, people, vehicles, animals, cups, containers, and funnels. Let children's interests determine the table's contents.

MUSICAL PAINTING: Using old sectioned baby plates, ice cube trays, or muffin tins, create a pallet of paint and place them between two easels, either next to an old white sheet spread out on the floor or by butcher paper hung securely on a wall. Let children converse about painting possibilities: "What should I paint? What are you going to paint?" Offer various shades and colors of paint, and play music—reggae, blue-grass, jazz, Latin, or classical—while the children are painting. Experiment with both slow tempos and upbeat sounds. Instruct the budding Picassos to paint what they hear the music "saying." Enhance musical painting by offering colorful painting hats or berets, as well as a variety of paintbrushes. Here are some paintbrush ideas:

- fingers
- spray bottles
- pastry brushes
- back brushes
- makeup brushes
- kitchen utensils
- watercolor wands, in which the paint is right in the sponge (watercolor wands and additional *Blick* art materials are available online, or call 800-828-4548)
- dried corncobs
- craft sticks
- eyedroppers
- gloves, latex-free or yellow rubber
- clean roll-on deodorant bottles
- small feather dusters
- cotton swabs
- ice cubes—before freezing them insert a craft stick as a handle
- plastic spatulas
- pumpkin or watermelon rinds with a secured fork handle

- broccoli stems

- wadded up cloth tied to a tongue depressor

- shaving cream brushes

- toothbrushes

- sponges of all shapes and sizes—synthetic sea sponges can add pizzazz to painting projects (www.eNasco.com/earlylearning)

- sponge hair rollers, with a clothespin clipped on for a quick handle

- rolling pins

- puzzle pieces with securely glued-on handles

- paint scrapers

- foam rollers (www.dickblick.com)

- floppy brushes (www.dickblick.com)

- supersized paintbrushes (www.dickblick.com)

Other musical painting ideas include displaying interesting art prints at the children's eye level around the easels—Van Gogh's Irises series is a fantastic choice. Paint possibilities are endless—thick pudding, colored funny foam, or homemade slime, gak, goop, or gunk . . . whatever! Be creative in individualizing musical painting experiences for a child who dabbles.

WET CHUNKY CHALK PLAY: Allow a child who dabbles and a zealous playmate to play with several sticks of chalk outside on the sidewalk or playground asphalt. For a novel chalk activity, toss the sticks in a large tub or gallon bucket of colored and scented water. Use smocks for wet chunky chalk play (old men's shirts make quick smocks). Add clean sand, rice, or other toss-ins to the water for increased sensory value. Add large sponges to the bucket so the two children can clean up afterward. Wringing out oversized sponges is great muscle work. Make plastic cups, ladles, bowls, and measuring cups available as well. As always, consider allergies with chalk play. Water play with chalk is a fabulous *supervised* tactile-sense activity.

Following are ideas to enhance wet chunky chalk play:

- Put additional objects, such as foam numbers or letters, in the bucket to be "fished" out with a small net. Add homemade "magnetic" fish with corresponding fishing poles.

- Toss in Mr. Potato Head pieces for the children to scoop out with their hands and assemble on its body. Add colored ice cubes to the bucket for pizzazz.

- Add bubbles and silly string to the big bucket of water play.

- Let the children use chalk to write on large, spread-out pieces of fabric, such as tablecloths. The use of different surfaces is ideal for chalk play. Use wallpaper, bubble wrap, dark paper, cardboard boxes, bricks, and, of course, the sidewalk.

- Visit Kodo Kids at www.kodokids.com for an introduction to the Chalk Spinner, a round spinning block of chalkboard made especially for budding creative minds.

HOT POTATO: Hot Potato is a quick, traditional game capable of working several of the senses, especially the vestibular, tactile, and proprioceptive (recall the triad approach on page 18). Hot Potato is an easy, impromptu behavioral-redirection game in which anything can become the potato. To play the game, designate the "potato." Try a small ball (Koosh, Nerf), a water balloon, a beanbag, a crumbled paper sack, a wadded up sock, or a knotted fabric texture like satin or Velcro. Toss the tater back and forth, up high, down low, and around and around to music. Explain to players that the tater is hot to the touch and they shouldn't be caught holding it. Rather, they should toss it to another player as soon as possible. Visit www.eNasco.com/earlylearning for a Squeeze the Hot Potato musical version. Additionally, don't be afraid to try other traditional games, such as jacks, marbles, or pick-up sticks, which also allow everyone a turn.

Ms. Lilly
SI Play Tip

A fun chant to add to a game of Hot Potato is *"Hot Potato, Hot Potato going all around. Where it stops, nobody knows. You are tatered out—o-u-t!"*

Keep the Atmosphere Noncompetitive and Orderly

For children experiencing a dabbling play challenge, it is essential to establish a relaxed learning environment with structure. The classroom atmosphere should encourage the child who dabbles to become a more active and eager learner. To accomplish this, the environment needs to remain noncompetitive and orderly. Here are five helpful tips (suitable for all play challenges) to obtain such a goal:

1. Limit group size for a dabbling child. Children who dabble often get lost in big groups. Smaller groups work best to prompt their play.

2. Keep classroom instructions and procedures simple and on a literal level. Avoid drawn-out directions. Use sensory integration in the procedures.

3. Do not compare a child's ideas and work to another child's. Children are like snowflakes: no two are alike.

4. Organize and design the classroom environment for acceptable behavior. Ask yourself, "Is the room crowded with unnecessary and distracting toys and furniture? What type of behavior does the room's layout promote?"

5. Have developmentally appropriate expectations. As educators, we need to continually offer and encourage high and positive expectations for our students, not inappropriate ones. An inappropriate expectation may resemble a three-year-old made to sit at circle time for twenty minutes or a toddler expected to share a new classroom toy without an available duplicate.

Lock Directly into the Child's Personal Interests and Learning Style

Locking directly into a child's personal interests and learning style is similar to going to a smorgasbord and observing what the child selects to eat and how she eats it. Often referred to as differentiated instruction, teaching specifically to cater to every child's individual needs can be overwhelming—most teachers feel their plates overflow. Keep the following in mind as you attempt to lock into a dabbling child's personal interests and learning style.

1. Refer back to PLEAS C ME on pages 7–12. Look closely at the E at the end of the acronym, which denotes Howard Gardner's eight multiple intelligences. Which one best suits how the dabbling child thinks and learns?

2. What sort of activities does the child most enjoy? Which of the following activities helps the child learn best?

- reading books or watching videos

- having discussions as a class

- participating in drill games

- fiddling alone

- playing computer games

- doing crafts

- going to learning centers

3. What interests the child? Does Jimmy like tigers? Does Sarah like dolls? What's her favorite color? What outdoor equipment does he play on at recess?

Parent questionnaires are helpful in answering these three questions as well. Home-school partnerships are important for strengthening the growth and development of children. Connecting early with parents about their child in reassuring and positive ways will help tremendously when tough issues come along. Parents will more than likely trust you after you have clearly expressed an interest in their child. I strongly suggest sending a short questionnaire home at the beginning and middle of the school year. A sample parent questionnaire can be found in appendix D.

An Individual Play Plan . . . for a Dabbling Mia

See page 21 for a discussion about the rationale of an individual play plan. Developing an individual play plan for a child who dabbles will assist in guiding you to support, include, and review her strengths, needs, and current observable and measurable performance in the areas of play concern. An individual play plan is meant to help you decide which strategies to use and how best to adapt or modify them to suit the child and ultimately lessen the play challenge. A sample individual play plan for dabbling Mia follows.

INDIVIDUAL PLAY PLAN

Child's name: Mia

Age: 4 years old

Play challenge or concern:

Mia demonstrates an unwillingness to experiment and explore with presented play materials and age-appropriate peers.

How does the play challenge affect involvement and progress in the general curriculum? For preschoolers and younger children, how does the play challenge affect involvement and progress in appropriate activities?

During class playtime with age-appropriate peers and activities, Mia fails to consistently interact with her peers and fails to consistently engage with presented play materials.

Additional present levels of performance:

Mia does not verbally communicate with her peers during play.

Mia shows no interest in her peers or play materials during play.

Sample goal, benchmark, or short-term objectives:

Mia will increase and sustain her play persistence and communication with peers to five minutes on task.

Possible methods of measurement for Mia's goals:

- clinical observation of Mia's performance (Adult observation of children is one of the most powerful assessment tools.)

- anecdotal notes about Mia

- checklists

- rating scales

- products (samples of what Mia has produced)

- portfolios (items selected over time to show progress)

- audio and video tapes

- photographs

- journals

- informal interviews

- conversations

- conferences with parents or guardians

Sensory-integration strategies and activities attempted (briefly respond to each play activity):

The following activities were attempted with Mia to alleviate and redirect her unwillingness to experience and explore presented play materials with age-appropriate peers.

Date: June 6 Activity: Bug hunt (found on page 36)—Observation illustrated that Mia enjoyed the buddy system bug hunt. She was reluctant at first but initiated interaction when her eager play partner began lifting up rocks and loose sidewalk steps to unveil pill bugs. Mia demonstrated hearty conversation with her play buddy as they poked the insects with discovered twigs.

Date: July 17 Activity: Hamburger making (found on page 45)

Observation illustrated that Mia found hamburger making pleasurable. Mia formed eight mud balls and pretended to grill them. She spoke briefly about her father's BBQ grill at home with the other two children at the center.

Selection of activity and how it has benefited the child:

The two activities benefited Mia's communication and social skills. She was excited to share her experiences playing with the insects. Locking into Mia's personal interests and naturalistic learning style propelled her play.

Progress toward goals and objectives:

Mia is progressing toward her goal to sustain her play and communication skills with peers.

Has the child's goal been met?

Mia's goal to increase or sustain her play persistence and communication with peers has increased on average between ten and eleven minutes! Mia has met her play challenge goal!

Notes and comments on regression/progression:

Enhancing classroom play centers with creative play materials prompted Mia to play and converse with peers. Mia benefited from peer modeling and orderly centers. She quickly put everything back in its right place and asked if she could "go to the hamburger maker next time." Mia's progression was welcomed by her classmates; they asked her to make them hamburgers "tomorrow." Mia creatively added fries—thinly rolled mud mixed with yarn strips.

Wrapping Up

As you contemplate which strategies to use to entice a dabbling child, remember that children often delight in simple pleasures like gazing at an aquarium full of goldfish or fidgeting with a wad of gak, goop, or glue. Ultimately, the sensory strategies chosen should extend and enhance the dabbler's sense of play mastery and persistence. Supply imaginative materials with accompanied encouragement and lock directly into the child's unique formula for learning. Doing so will surely sustain play for a child who dabbles. Eventually, he will accept an invitation to "Come and play!"

Check out the following resources for additional sensory-integration play ideas for children who dabble.

Ants in Their Pants: Teaching Children Who Must Move to Learn by Aerial Cross

Everyday Early Learning: Easy and Fun Activities and Toys Made from Stuff You Can Find around the House by Jeff A. Johnson with Zoë Johnson

I Love Dirt! 52 Activities to Help You and Your Kids Discover the Wonders of Nature by Jennifer Ward

Learning Games: Exploring the Senses through Play by Jackie Silberg

Make Your Own Playdough, Paint, and Other Craft Materials: Easy Recipes to Use with Young Children by Patricia Caskey

Motivation is when your dreams put on work clothes.

—Parkes Robinson

Steering the Roaming Child to Play

We all know what roaming means—to go from place to place without purpose or direction: to wander—to borrow *Merriam-Webster's* definition. But what does it mean when we say a child has a roaming play challenge? Children with a roaming play challenge consistently wander or meander about during playtime. Children who consistently roam a classroom during playtime threaten vital play and skill-building acquisition experiences necessary for progressing academic, social, emotional, and cognitive development. This chapter focuses on children with roaming play challenges. These children resemble roaming Jamal in the example that follows.

Roaming Jamal

Afternoon center time is under way. Jamal's teacher has placed him at the snack center, where he will be making "ants on a log" with raisins, peanut butter, and celery. Within minutes of sitting down at the center table, Jamal is out of his chair, roaming the playroom. Although quiet and tentative, he moves about the classroom touching things unobtrusively, humming and clicking his tongue, while watching the other children play. Jamal is not causing any immediate or disruptive trouble, but his continual roaming is problematic. He is not engaging in consistent play. Jamal is demonstrating a roaming play challenge.

A child who demonstrates the following behaviors persistently, in a consistent pattern over an extended period of time, may be struggling with a roaming play challenge:

- The child spends an abnormal amount of time wandering aimlessly around the classroom or play area.

- The child is consistently uninvolved with peers or materials during playtime.

- The child consistently meanders on the edge of play, only watching fellow playmates.

- The child flits from play space to play space.

- The child drifts around touching and investigating things already investigated over and over and over.

Reasons a Child May Roam

A child may roam in play for a variety of reasons:

- The child may be experiencing a developmental delay, causing frustration or difficulty in play. Refer to pages 26–27 for further explanation of what a developmental delay might resemble.

- The child may be unsure of what to do during play. Even after specific directions have repeatedly been given, a child may remain unclear of a play activity's procedures and purpose. It is important to capitalize on the child's individual learning style. Recall the last E in PLEAS C ME from chapter 1. A combined learning approach, such as visual, auditory, and tactile-kinesthetic, may be needed for the child to understand. Use pictures, symbols, words, or even simple flowcharts to present ideas in a variety of ways.

- The child may not want to play with the available play materials offered at the time. Often children are reluctant to play in a center or activity simply because something else has captured their fancy. This may be the answer to why a child is roaming from one center to the next, or continually roaming to a particular room location.

- The child may be "stuck" and unable to get play started. She may be unable to gain social entry into the play activity. A child may roam because she doesn't know how else to extend the play materials or center activities. In short, she has exhausted all the play possibilities she knows and starts roaming to entertain herself.

- The child may not understand the "hidden agenda" of the play the other children are engaged in and feels more comfortable and secure watching from the outskirts of the activity. Children come from all walks of life. Cultures and family traditions vary. A child may roam because he is not familiar with the play. It may be different from his family culture or traditions.

- The child may lack self-confidence and intrinsic motivation to press forward in play. Refer to pages 27–28 for explanation regarding the significance of intrinsic motivation to prompt play.

Key Intervention Guidelines

To steer a roaming child to play, use developmentally appropriate activities, creative play centers, and sensory activities wrapped in continual encouragement. Establish physical play boundaries and provide a detailed play plan, preferably in guided steps. Buddy play at classroom centers with minimal distractions is beneficial for roamers. Regardless of the play challenge, journaling is also helpful, as is looking closely at a child's individual PLEAS C ME information. Journal in detailed notes about when and how intensely children roam. Doing so will help you discover patterns or uncover root causes.

Key intervention strategies for steering a roaming child to play are:

- Plan activities that are developmentally appropriate.

- Help a child who roams to select play options.

- Help a child who roams to sustain play with continual encouragement. Check in and out of the play.

- Make use of play areas that have fewer distractions.

- Establish physical play boundaries.

- Designate a classroom or outside play path for a child who roams to rove.

- Write a play plan with the child who roams.

- Support the start of the child's play with prompting and prodding. Model the play activity. Refer to pages 31–33 for creative-thinking strategies to prompt play.

- Pair a child who roams with a play buddy. Refer to pages 44–49 for examples of play buddy activities.

The coming pages present extraordinary ideas and activities to steer a roaming child toward, in, or through play. Keep the following objectives in mind while wading through the ideas.

1. Clearly look at the definition of a roaming play challenge, possible reasons for the child's roaming, and intervention strategies for a roaming child. Sometimes adjusting or tweaking small classroom conditions easily remedies a roaming play challenge.

2. Review the key intervention strategies on pages 59–60 for steering a roaming child to play. The intervention strategy needed may be staring right back at you. Recall the three principles of sensory integration from page 13. It is important to frequently revisit the three principles of sensory integration to reestablish the purpose of positioning a child to succeed within sensory-rich activities that are pleasurable and that shout, "Come and play!"

3. Rule out any basic health, vision, hearing, or learning disability possibilities that could be causing a roaming play challenge.

4. If the roaming persists or increases in intensity (after several documented intervention attempts), hold a conference with the parent or guardian. Consultation with an outside community resource may be needed. Remember, early intervention is key!

5. As with all classroom, home, or center learning experiences, put safety, health, and age appropriateness at the forefront of all activities. Additionally, keep play opportunities individualized, nonthreatening, and unforced.

Sensory-Integration Strategies to Steer a Roaming Child to Play

The following pages of strategies are useful in steering roaming children to play. The activities are imaginative and easy, and supplies are simple and accessible. The strategies can be modified to remedy other play challenges and simplified or extended for student need and interest. Roaming children will blend learning and the fun generated from the listed sensory strategies.

Plan Developmentally Appropriate Activities

Planning developmentally appropriate activities is pertinent for addressing any play challenge. Developmentally appropriate refers to how children develop and learn and to planned classroom curriculum and strategies for educating them (Kostelnik 1993, 74). Matching activities to a child's developmental level is imperative. Play activities and materials that are too easy or too difficult may lead to roaming.

Keep the following in mind when planning developmentally appropriate play activities that incorporate the seven senses of sensory integration for steering a child who roams to play.

1. Allow roamers regular time each day for free play, especially constructive play with lots of interesting *things* with which to construct interesting *things*. Be consistent with rules of play, remembering that free play denotes play of choice, not free time to roam. See appendix C for a list of constructive playthings that are creative and age appropriate.

2. Provide a child who roams ample time daily for outdoor play adventures in nature. Designate play boundaries.

3. Incorporate learning centers that are simple and self-explanatory for a child who roams. A block center is an example of a simple and self-explanatory center. Blocks can be wooden, cardboard brick, or foam. Regardless of type, blocks are straightforward and simple. Follow these tips for a simply structured and sensory-oriented block center:

- Use a carpeted area for noise control (with wooden blocks).

- Make play props available (for example, plastic animals, toy vehicles, and boards for ramps).

- Enhance the center with roads designed with masking tape (add homemade traffic signs).

- Incorporate curriculum concepts (for instance, if you're studying Africa, add miniature animals native to Africa and brown paper or fabric to represent desert sand).

- Add books with photographs of large buildings or towers (post a picture of the Great Wall of China in the block area).

- Make, review, and post signs ("Blocks are for building, not for throwing" or "Not finished: Please do not knock over").

4. Using multiple intelligences, provide a child who roams with several ways to approach and tackle a task. Like adults, children do not all learn the same way or have the same strengths and weaknesses. Thank goodness! For example, if you're teaching children about insects, include an oral discussion, a visual display, and a hands-on experience with bugs in jars. Catering to all learning styles in a classroom makes for effective sensory-integrated teaching.

5. Guide a child who roams to and through play. Refrain from dictating *how* to play. Keep your role balanced:

- Offer, encourage, and facilitate play—set the stage, so to speak.

- Enhance play regularly with new ideas and creative things.

- Aid children in figuring out play obstacles on their own as much as possible.

- Model playfulness.

- Share play.

- Talk with children about their play (Schirrmacher 2002, 53).

6. Teach thematically (cross curriculum). In other words, the curriculum should carry over into a roaming child's free playtime. For example, the alphabet and its sounds can be taught through hands-on letter books. The books start with the letter *C* and progress to *O, G, A, D, S,* etc. The books build

on one another as children learn to blend sounds and read words—*dog, gag, sag,* and *dad,* for example. (Similar book activities can be found online at www.preschoolrainbow.org/alphabet.htm.) Some sounds require a week's time. Others, such as the letter *S,* can take two weeks. Depending on the letter, teach thematically by the week or two weeks. Send parents a calendar and newsletter explaining the letter that will be studied and its corresponding activities. *Hands-on Alphabet Activities for Young Children: A Whole Language Plus Phonetics Approach to Reading* by Roberta Seckler Brown and Susan Carey is a wonderful resource for collecting calendar ideas.

The following list shows examples of letter *S* theme activities and centers:

- Writing: Children work on printing the letter *S* during class time and at an afternoon center (in a variety of mediums).

- Math: Children identify spheres and cylinders. Discuss the beginning sounds of these words. Carry the concept over into a science center with a variety of containers for pouring water, sifting, and measuring.

- Show-and-tell: Children bring in a favorite item that starts with an *S.*

- Science: Children learn about snakes that are native to their state.

- Social studies: Children study the southern states of America.

- Centers: Adapt centers or introduce new ones related to the letter *S.* For example, set up a simple spirograph center, a stamp and stencil center, or a snack center.

7. Sing a lot, especially during play commencement or transitioning periods. Use imaginative props, creative fingerplays, vibrant sign language, or catchy voice fluctuation to enhance classroom singing.

8. Integrate sensory teaching-delivery methods for prodding play (remember, not all children learn the same way). Use individualized focusing activities and prompts that motivate the child. An example of a sensory-integrated delivery method with individualized focusing potential is using a fuzzy hand puppet that catches the child's fancy. Something as simple as a

colorful puppet can stimulate and motivate a child to proceed with and sustain play.

9. Keep play activities open-ended and engaging. A significant difference exists between close-ended, overly structured (often teacher-directed) play and play that is open-ended and engaging (often child-oriented).

OPEN-ENDED PLAY IS	CLOSE-ENDED PLAY IS
• unique and original	• rote and routine
• self-expressed	• imitative (copying is involved)
• process oriented	• product oriented
• pleasing to children	• pleasing to adults
• messy	• clean and constructed

Beware of activities masquerading as play, which may look like coloring-book pages, dot-to-dot sheets, and cut-and-paste worksheets. These are close-ended activities involving very low-level thinking and do not promote sensory integration.

10. Model a genuine passion for play. Enthusiasm is contagious!

Ms. Lilly
SI Play Tip

Children are skilled at transforming everyday objects into useful and creative play props. Provide props and prompts for sensory-integration play activities that are realistic and multipurpose. For example, provide real shampoo bottles (washed out and cleaned) filled with colored and scented water for a hair salon center. Add big vibrating hairbrushes, fluffy terry cloth hand towels, bright colored hairpins, barrettes, and dolls with lots of wild and woolly hair to assume the role of "customer." Boxes can become playhouses or appliances. A bandanna can be part of a pirate costume or a baby doll blanket. A Frisbee can be a plate, a paint pallet, or a stepping-stone.

Help a Roaming Child Select Play Options

Ever take a small child to an ice cream shop with thirty-one or more flavors? Speaking from experience, it can be a trying event. Although children need to learn how to make choices, too many choices can quickly overwhelm them. Children with roaming challenges often need support in making play choices and often cooperate more effectively when given narrow choices. Depending on the child, it might be helpful to offer two play choices—"this" or "that." "Eduardo, you may play at the block center ("this") or the painting center ("that"). Which center do you choose?"

Make this or that choices either a lot alike or very different. This or that play choices that are a lot alike help to narrow choices down for children who refuse or putter with play options. This or that play choices that are very different cater to individual natures and dispositions needing a smidgen of affirming control in play choice. After a while, you'll discover the play choices each child prefers. Several play choices for a child who roams follow.

DRAMATIC PLAY CENTER: Toss old clothing and theme costumes (firefighter, doctor, nurse, farmer, airline pilot, etc.) in a large, brightly colored designated box. Add age-appropriate and safe accessories, such as costume jewelry; lab coats; bathrobes; hats of all sorts, sizes, and textures; gloves; necklaces; goggles; belts; neckties; silky scarves; pretend medical kits with real gauze; and, of course, a floor-length mirror for admiring finished dressing. Literacy props, such as menus, clipboards with paper, food ordering forms, and pretend prescription and phone message pads are creative additions as well. By putting a tennis ball on top of a thick stick, a microphone can be quickly made for aspiring vocalists. For multicultural connections, add eating and cooking utensils from different cultures, including chopsticks, wooden spoons, ladles, saucepans, strainers, woks, tortilla presses, tea balls, teapots (with matching cups), whisks, and fry pans. Be sure to add a variety of baby-tending items, such as a stroller, infant sling, and Native American cradleboard. Stitched or cloth dolls representing countries from across the globe make great additions.

GADGET CENTER: Many children find it fascinating to unscrew and take apart old appliances such as toasters and radios. Garage sales are hot spots for effectively equipping a gadget center. As always, consider age appropriateness with gadgets. Here are some gadget ideas to significantly sustain a roaming child's play potential:

- broken clocks
- old rotary telephones
- unusable cameras
- nuts and bolts
- washers and screws
- locks with linking keys
- levers and pulleys
- small ramps with small toy cars
- an assortment of kaleidoscopes
- simple scales (balance, platform, or digital)
- measuring tapes and rulers

Ms. Lilly
SI Play Tip

A dramatic play area filled with a variety of visually patterned and textured dress-up clothes is wonderful for inspiring play possibilities. Encourage role-playing and independence while providing time to practice real-life dressing skills, such as buttoning, buckling, snapping, zipping, tying a bow, lacing, clasping, and rolling up sleeves. Manual dexterity boards and vests for practicing such skills are available online. If you're feeling exceptionally creative and brave, allow face paint crayons in a dramatic play center.

Ms. Lilly
SI Play Tip

A quick way to beef up a science center is to add colorful magnetic wands of varying weights and accompanying items. They'll help children easily explore the world of magnetism. Oversized horseshoe magnets are fun too.

Children can be taught the basics of measuring with rulers through *measuring worms*—squishy, multicolored worms for counting, sorting, and measuring. *Inchworms* are also great for snapping into flexible chains for learning concepts of width, length, and circumference. Find these at Nasco, www.eNasco .com/earlylearning.

Ms. Lilly
SI Play Tip

Let students make fingerprints with finger paint called pumpkin "goo." It is an awesome sensory experience! You'll need a pumpkin or two. Cut off the tops. With the children, scoop out the goo from inside the pumpkin. Let children play with the goo on cookie sheets or wax paper. Have them remove the seeds from the goo.

- screwdrivers

- small hammers

- wire cutters

- magnets in all shapes and sizes

- goofy goggles

BUBBLE PLAY: Fill several big buckets and pots full of sudsy water. The more bubble foam, the better—children enjoy playing with it! To pump up the sensory value with froth and fizz, add baking soda and vinegar. Have the child who roams carry the water-weighted buckets to designated outside play spots. Put bubble wands of several sizes, whistles, plastic dishes, dolls, and toys in the buckets. Toss a few clean flyswatters in too—they make great bubble wands. Let the child who roams individually explore the wet bubbly play. Water activities should *always* be supervised.

PUMPKIN PLAY: This is a seasonal activity to do when pumpkins are available. Spread newspaper on a large table or outside on playground asphalt. Cut off the tops of several pumpkins of different sizes and shapes. Let the roaming child choose a pumpkin to clean out and decorate. Have him put the slippery, slimy, mushy insides (and seeds to sort later) in a huge pot. Make gloves, shovels, markers, and other play items available. Allow the child who roams to steer his pumpkin play.

Help a Child Who Roams Sustain Play with Continual Encouragement

The power of words is enormous and pivotal for small children. Words spoken by a parent or educator can literally make or break a child's social, emotional, and academic development. Always choose words appropriately and effectively, especially regarding play challenge regression or progression. Sensory-integrated play activities combined with effective words of encouragement can tremendously prolong a roaming child's play. A few quick ideas and examples capable of working wonders for the roaming child who is stumped in play follow:

- Vibrant hand gestures or props: Mandy has been on task for five minutes at a combined art and science center. She is frustrated because her collected leaves from an afternoon nature walk won't "stay sticked" to her art collage. Mandy is preparing to roam. When you notice this behavior, walk over to her with a puppet prop and ask vibrantly, "How else could we get those wonderful leaves you collected to stick?"

- Individualized music choices: Individualized music can be used as encouragement by allowing a roaming child to select his favorite tunes to listen to during class. "Ashley, pick a CD for us all to listen to as we work today."

- Animated voice inflections: Dalton is at the playdough table playing persistently with newly added accessories. Eyeing the tortilla press that another student is working with, Dalton suddenly grabs it out of the child's hands. A tug of war ensues. Act on the squabble by asking for the toy and then using an animated voice inflection with your question, "How else could you have gotten the tortilla press from Jaden without *hurting Jaden's feelings*?" Emphasize "hurting Jaden's feelings."

- Direct eye contact: With words, signals, or a combination of the two, use direct eye contact to help encourage and sustain a child who roams in play. Look at her directly and give a thumbs-up or a nod of the head to encourage her to stay engaged and on task. A soft pat on the back and a smile work as well.

There is a difference between effective and ineffective encouragement. All the sensory props and strategies in the world won't make much difference if encouragement is continually given without meaning or connection to the child. Ineffective encouragement is praise without direct association to a child, his actions, improvements, or, in a roaming child's case, sustenance *in* or *to* play. As an educator, you will discover a fine line exists for each and every child regarding praise dosage. While you don't want a child to become dependent on you or for false praise to prolong playfulness, shoot to build inner (intrinsic) motivation. Whether this is achieved for a roamer by renewing fresh play ideas or tacking new perspectives on old ones is your call as the educator.

Let's look again at roaming Jamal to display a point about encouragement. Today Jamal has managed to lengthen his play by two minutes longer than yesterday. He has playfully produced a massive block tower complete with an imaginative

Ms. Lilly
SI Play Tip

Whispering can grab a child's attention, redirect, and resolve "stumped" or frustrated play. Try whispering softly, "The tortilla press will be at this center for a whole week. I promise you'll get a turn with it."

drawbridge and surrounding townspeople made from wads of playdough. The gain in Jamal's play performance and longevity is huge. Jamal's teacher expresses, "What a great job!" Although the words are praiseworthy and well intended, they more than likely are motivationally ineffective to Jamal and his play challenge goals.

Effective encouragement assists children in becoming intrinsically motivated by focusing directly on their strengths and reinforcing positive behaviors. Effective encouragement focuses on efforts, not results. When proclaiming to Jamal how proud of his work she was, his teacher should have linked Jamal's block creation to his prolonged play efforts, using his name for direct connection, squatting to Jamal's level for direct eye contact, and extending play with a prodding question: "Jamal! Wow! What a grand tower you made. I am so proud of you for working hard at building such a wonderful tower. Who lives in this magnificent tower you built?" Understanding and using effective encouragement is essential for addressing the roaming child's play challenge.

Make Use of Play Areas with Fewer Distractions

Start a roaming child's play at a classroom center with few distractions. Partition off an area with curtains or a screen, if possible, for a more private, absorbed play session. Garden lattices, canopies, and shelves are useful in keeping play areas away from distraction and main classroom traffic. Ideas for quiet, absorbing play centers follow.

BOARD GAME CENTER: Set up a cozy area with shelves of games, such as Chutes and Ladders, Don't Break the Ice, Connect Four, and Cootie. Thoroughly discuss and post age-appropriate play rules. Chaos and conflict can ensue quickly when play rules are unclear.

FINE-MOTOR ACTIVITIES: Offer an assortment of fine-motor activities in an area sectioned off with beanbags. Here are some fine-motor activity suggestions:

- textured lacing exercises

- textured stencils for tracing

- textured finger stampers (www.centerenterprises.com)

- sets of punch-outs in all shapes and sizes

- jewelry for beading

- 3-D or magnetic puzzles

PUPPET THEATER: Puppets are outstanding for emerging language skills. Set up a simple box for an easy, impromptu puppet theater. Add sensory sock puppets, stick puppets, box puppets, plastic foam cup puppets, glove puppets, paper plate puppets, tissue tube puppets, or brown paper bag puppets. For reasonably priced, extraordinary puppet products, including ones that blink and give detailed attention to facial expression (excellent for working with anxious, detached, and rejected children), visit www.puppetsinc.com.

COMPUTER CENTER: Allow interactive computer play with accompanying headphones. Cover the headphones with earmuffs if background noise is problematic for a child who roams.

LIBRARY CENTER: Chair pockets for storing library books tied behind a child's desk will promote *anytime* reading. Make books of all types available by situating shelves around the following:

- big comfy pillows

- vibrating pillows

- ottomans, hassocks, bolsters (www.safespaceconcepts.com)

- beanbags

- glider rocking chairs

- old inner tubes (for gentle bouncing)

- big decorated boxes to veg out in

  Stock the library center with a variety of books for a roaming child to choose from:

- beginning reader books, such as those by Dr. Seuss

- simple concept books that illustrate numbers, colors, animals, or opposites

- poetry books

Ms. Lilly
SI Play Tip

For lacing or craft activities, shoelaces or yarn can be used in place of string. Wind masking tape around the tips for greater stability. Make lacing cards extra stiff and manageable by cutting designs from vinyl flooring. Make holes with a hole punch.

Ms. Lilly
SI Play Tip

Here are four fabulous reasons to use finger puppets for sensory play:

- Finger puppets and rhymes are perfect partners in early education.

- Finger puppets are attention grabbing for many children with play challenges.

- Finger puppets add magic and drama to everyday class activities and routines.

- Finger puppets can enhance every part of the curriculum, including reading, science, music, art, and math. Visit Artfelt Puppet System at www.artfelt.net for a variety of adorably realistic felt-board finger puppets.

- books that appeal to the senses—"scratch and sniff," "feel the textured fabric," "pull the tab," or "pop-up" books

- musical books that play tunes when opened

- Leap Frog books or other Leap Frog interactive products

- children's magazines, such as *Ranger Rick, National Geographic Kids,* or *Highlights* (*Highlights* magazine now offers *Highlights High Five,* especially for two- to six-year-olds.)

- homemade books (baggie books, or memory picture books made by the child during class)

- flannel board stories (Lay out a flannelboard with connecting pieces for the child who roams to tell inspirational stories. *Goldilocks and the Three Bears* is a simple flannelboard story to make out of felt.)

Establish Physical Boundaries

Maria Montessori developed a theory that children learn best by being active and by continually "doing." Roaming children are active—it's the "doing" in play they often overlook. If there is no intervention, a child who roams can wander right past dynamic play opportunities. To assist the roaming child in becoming a more self-directed player, establish tight physical boundaries within the classroom play spaces. Physically walk through the room and discuss play boundaries with roamers. For a small-scale play boundary, think of a plate with a rim. The rim boundary keeps play objects, such as marbles, on the plate and within sight and reach. To achieve a more restricted play area on a larger scale, use the following ideas.

BOXES: Define a roaming child's play space by establishing "boxed-in" boundaries. Remove any staples or tape from boxes. Adults should always do the cutting of boxes for play. Creative ideas for boxes follow.

- Beach boxes: With duct, mechanical, or masking tape, section off a "beach" area. Fill a low-sided box with a small amount of sand (see page 112 for sensory sand options). Add measuring cups, shovels, and pails for an indoor beach adventure. Display different sized seashells.

Put a drop cloth down for catching sand. Visit Children's Factory at www.childrensfactory.com for a plush beach ball lounger to accent any beach box play area.

- Body boxes: A body box is a box that appears as if it were made specifically for a roaming child. She'll fit snuggly inside. Fill a body box with packing peanuts and let her sit inside and play. You'll need to supervise play in body boxes, of course.

- Box bowling: Use duct tape to section off an area in the classroom as a bowling lane. Discuss the lane boundaries with roamers. Use several shoe boxes and a tennis ball to muster up a quick game of box bowling.

- Buildings: Large boxes can become a variety of buildings—a grocery store, playhouse, post office, fire station, or hospital—for center play with boundaries. Stock each play building with corresponding and creative supplies; for example, in the grocery store stock plastic food items and have a cash register stashed with paper cash.

- Campgrounds: Turn a big box into a tent. Roll out a sleeping bag. Add small snacks in a wicker picnic basket and a water canteen. Give a roaming child a flashlight for inside!

- Cars: Transform a dryer box into a school bus, fire truck, or racecar. Small children enjoy sitting in boxes and wiggling, "vrooming" forward in them. This is excellent physical exercise.

- Caves: After cutting an entryway, give a roaming child a flashlight to explore inside the pretend cavern. Drape a blanket over the box for added cave darkness, or turn a box upside down and cut a big hole in the top for an underground submarine effect.

- Playhouses: Refrigerator boxes make fabulous playhouses. Cut out a door and windows. Add rooms to the house with a few blankets thrown over several chairs. Big pillows make convenient walls. Or, turn a playhouse into a barn. Be imaginative.

- Tunnels: Connect a few sturdy boxes for a crawl-through tunnel. Large plastic trash cans can also be used as

Ms. Lilly
SI Play Tip

Turn a physical boundary or tunnel for a roaming child into a spectacular adventure. Connect and decorate large boxes to create a starry space station. Visit www.BabyScholars.com for a listing of space tunnel and tent products to stimulate little minds with sensory play.

tunnels by cutting out their bottoms and connecting each end to end. Drape colorful comforters over the top as a canopy for holding the boxes and trash cans in place. The weighted blankets will darken and secure the boxes during movements inside. Cut holes in the boxes for a "skylight." Toss a few squishy toy bugs, soft pillows, or even sticky contact paper inside the tunnel. Encourage children to move forward and backward through the tunnel with a flashlight.

TAPE: Colored electrical, masking, or duct tape can be used to make physical boundaries for roamers. "Johnny, your play area is in the big blue taped box. Do you see it? Let's walk around it together."

ROPE: Rope off play areas with sturdy nylon rope. Set up a pretend outdoor restaurant center with tables, chairs, aprons, placemats, and ordering pads. Drape blue sheets over the sides of the rope for an imaginative ocean-side scene. A creatively roped off airport center complete with aisled chairs, suitcases, and tickets for punching is another idea. Reinforce the rope boundary for the child who roams with tape about two inches outside the rope. Be inventive. Rope seasonal lights around play areas.

CURTAINS: Gather old curtains from thrift stores and set up a tepee in a classroom corner. Widely pin back an opening for full inside supervised viewing. On the outside of the curtains, string seasonal lights. Set up a pretend birthday party with hats and party accessories inside the play area. Have a child who roams and a play buddy wrap pretend presents with a variety of paper (see pages 39–40 for an assortment of paper options).

SITUATE TOYS: Purposely arrange, angle, and corner toys and furniture to form physical boundaries for play. Use window seats, cabinets, countertops, lofts, stepping stools, potted plants, portable screens, and dividers to close off areas or use as entry and exit ways. Think cozy cove or hidden hideaway. Set up a kitchen area complete with box-made appliances such as an oven, dishwasher, and sink. Add colorful hanging fabric to close the kitchen off for focused and cooperative play.

MATS OR BLANKETS: Plan play on a large, tactile shock-absorbing mat, quilted blanket, or comforter. Mats can also be folded for a tunnel effect. Large area play rugs work well too. Visit www.carpetsforkids.com for dazzling possibilities. Pretend a large blanket or mat is a magic carpet, and inform the roaming child he can choose wherever he wants to go. Place paper and printing utensils on the imaginative ride, and allow the roaming child to draw his flying adventures. Or use an Etch A Sketch, Draw and Write Touch Board, or Color-Changing Touch Board (www .lakeshorelearning.com).

WADING POOLS: Wading pools or ball pits are ideal for making play boundaries for roaming children. Have the child who roams find hidden treasures in the pool or pit. Clean troughs also work well. Here are some items you can use to fill the pool, pit, or trough:

- beans
- colored craft cotton balls
- craft feathers
- popcorn kernels
- rice
- small, slimy-feeling balls
- small, tactile toys
- squishy, squashy sponges
- Styrofoam peanuts
- textured bumpy balls
- sensory balls (brightly colored balls with a variety of textures such as ridges, nubs, and indentions—visit www.lakeshorelearning.com for sensory ball sets)

GAZEBOS: Transform a gazebo into a "fab lab" play area. Set up science experiments, sprout plants, hang bird feeders, host an afternoon picnic, or offer a variety of seating options for scientific picture book reading. Set out recycling bins and have children sort cardboard, paper, and glass products. If the gazebo is large enough, hang a hammock. During the warmer months of the school year, hatch chicks or ducks with a large incubator situated safely on the gazebo lab.

Ms. Lilly
SI Play Tip

Giving one another "blanket rides" is a fabulous physical play exercise that increases muscle tone and balancing skills. Have a child sit on a hefty comforter or blanket and allow another child to pull it along the floor. Set up small cones for the children to pull up to and weave in and out of. A sturdy box or laundry basket can be used instead of a blanket for this activity (Sher 2004, 105).

Ms. Lilly
SI Play Tip

Let children color outdoors in an empty and dry wading pool. Cut a large piece of butcher paper to fit the pool's circumference. Allow children to sit in the pool with a variety of coloring utensils and stencils to use.

Move the hatchery laboratory indoors when the weather isn't cooperative.

HEARTY PLANTS: Fast-growing, hearty plants, such as cornstalks and sunflowers work well to define outdoor play boundaries for children. Climbing plants can be monitored and used to create boundaries for a play refuge as well.

Make a Play Path

A play path is a purposefully situated trail of play inside or outside a classroom. Use lines of colored tape or flags to mark the route of the play path. Just as baseball players must advance from base to base, children must advance to points along the play path. Use numbers or symbols to help children progress from one point

JAMAL'S PLAY PATH

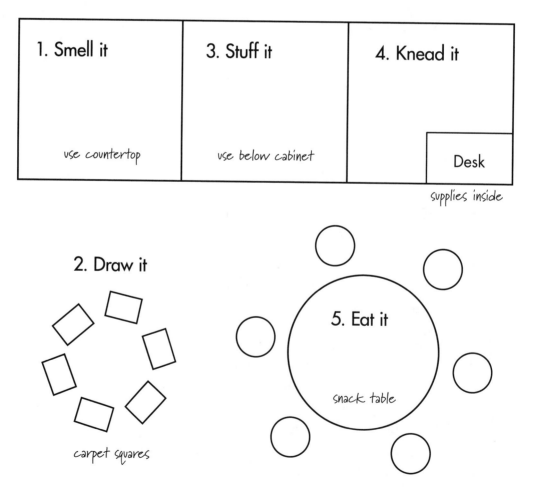

to the next, and offer a variety of sitting features along the path, such as rocking chairs, beanbags, rugs, and oversized pillows. Refer to Jamal's Play Path on page 74 for a sample indoor play path.

1. Smell it: Place cotton balls soaked in a variety of scents and seasoning in small cups. Have the roaming child try to match the scent in the cup to a displayed picture. For example, match peppermint-scented cotton balls to a picture of a candy cane. In place of cups, you can also use small plastic water bottles wrapped in colored paper for a more "secretive" effect. Children unscrew the tops and try to match the smell to pictures. Use intense scents, such as vinegar, steak sauce, honey, garlic salt, baby powder, root beer extract, and facial cream.

2. Draw it: Make sandpaper stencils of all sizes and shapes available. Let the child who roams trace them while sitting on situated carpet squares.

3. Stuff it: Completely clear out a bottom classroom cabinet for a "stuff it" stop along a play path. Fill an assortment of containers and boxes with various things for a roaming child to stock, sort, and stuff in the cabinet. Ideas for materials to stock and stuff include:

   - empty cereal boxes of all sizes to stock (cut up a few cereal box covers into puzzles; put in plastic bags)

   - coffee tins (metal or plastic) and egg and milk cartons to situate in the cabinet

   - cigar boxes filled with assorted fabric scraps to sort

   - empty (and clean) pill bottles, film containers, and spice bottles of all sizes to sort

   - oatmeal containers filled with rice and sealed tightly

   - butter tubs of all sizes filled with rocks and sealed tightly

   - plastic jars of all shapes and sizes with the lids in a bag for children to match and stock

   - detergent boxes empty or half full of rice (once again, securely sealed)

4. Knead it: Make a huge batch of thickly textured, scented playdough. Set out cookie cutters and different sized rolling pins. Have the child who roams knead the dough, roll the dough, and cut out cookies at a desk. Press it! Pound it! Flatten

it! Snake roll it! Just work it! This center can be transformed into "Pour it" by gathering a variety of liquids to pour. Children can compare and contrast maple syrup, colored water, cooking oil, vinegar, soy sauce, and strong coffee. Put liquids in an assortment of measuring pitchers (gallon, half-gallon, quart, pint, and cup sizes). Heavy-duty, lightweight plastic ones can be found online at www.eNasco.com. These are great for sensory-oriented class cooking projects too!

5. Eat it: At the end of the play path, set up a small snack center with a variety of foods, such as pretzels, tortilla strips, salsa, sliced bananas, ice water, and even spinach leaves. Toss in a few Pop Rocks candies or dry cereal to eat with chopsticks. Be creative. This center can be turned into "Taste it" by setting out a variety of sweet, sour, and salty foods. Later, you can incorporate spicy and bland foods to enhance the activity. Let children classify the foods according to tastes. Put the samples on individual plates for each child. Use craft sticks or plastic spoons for sampling. Sample foods might include lemon wedges, honey, carrot coins, chocolate chips, cheese chunks, and cottage cheese. Please always check for children with food allergies when using food experiences.

When producing a play path, keep the following in mind: A path without creative- and critical-thinking obstacles probably won't challenge a child. "Rock the child's boat" within a play path.

Additional play path ideas follow.

SENSORY STEPPING-STONES: Textured stepping-stones inside or outside of a classroom make outstanding sensory play paths for children who roam! Hobby stores offer flat stones that can be easily turned into pathways (options for flat stones can be viewed at www.Alibaba.com). Sturdy metal pie pans or old Frisbees make great pathway stones. Use a variety of other textures to create a sensory pathway. Try bricks, woodchips, mulch, gravel, sod patches, or flagstones. Textured balance beams and bars with inclines, steps, or crawl-over walls are excellent play path ideas. Tunnels or age-appropriate ramps can also enhance stepping-stone pathways indoors or out.

Visit www.lakeshorelearning.com for a Walk-the-Wave balance beam. It is all the fun of a traditional balance beam

Ms. Lilly
SI Play Tip
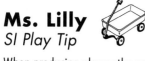

When producing play paths and obstacle courses, think back to grade school lessons about positional prepositions and action verbs. Use variety in directions:
- step *over* the bubble wrap
- crawl *across* the tires
- lean *against* the boxes
- skip *around* the chair
- tiptoe *behind* the bridge
- gallop *beside* the log
- go *down* the slide
- sit *inside* the barrel
- jump *off* the small stool
- run *on* the taped line
- jump *outside* the box
- slither *through* the cardboard tunnel
- scoot *under* the rope
- roll the ball *up* the slide

with curves and gradual height changes. Here are some other large-motor stepping-stone suggestions:

- Hilltops: Five "hilltops" in different heights that will inspire children to jump from top to top (www.sensoryedge.com).

- River Stones: These stones are inspired by those found in a river, with each side varying in steepness and difficulty (www.sensoryedge.com).

- Step-a-Logs: Connected logs with raised dots for safety and tactile stimulation (www.eNasco.com).

- Stepping Stilt Buckets: These buckets are a great challenge for walking on, or turn them over and fill them with a variety of sensory items, such as shaving cream, sand, or water (www.eNasco.com).

- Tactile Discs: Children are challenged to develop their sense of touch with hands and feet using tactile discs. Tactile discs are also great for blindfold games in which children have to rely on memory and touch recognition (www.kaplantoys.com).

A BOX PATH: Create an outside play path using sturdy boxes (photocopy paper boxes work well) and tubs. Old washtubs are hefty and strong and can be put above or in the ground. Decorate each container in bold colors and fill with sand, dirt, water, small aquarium pebbles, crunchy fall leaves, cotton balls, feathers, or squishy toy bugs. Situate the boxes in a circle or square. Have the child who roams walk in and out of the boxes barefoot, in socks, or in galoshes. Add music.

FALL LEAVES: Craft a trail of fall leaves on the playground for a roaming child to run through. Rustling leaves are not only pleasurable to touch, but also amazing to hear. Dampen the leaves for a more physical activity. (Dry leaves are not as heavy as wet leaves.)

CARPET TUBES: Large carpet flooring tubes can be acquired from carpet stores, sawed into sections, and turned into awesome obstacle courses for children to "putt-putt" balls through along a play path.

TIRE TRACKS: Construct a tire trail. Systematically lay out three to five tires and fill each with a variety of play options and

Ms. Lilly
SI Play Tip

When the weather is cooperative, not too hot or windy, set up a trike and wagon parade for children. Situate a flagged course on the playground. Place interactive stops (outdoor centers) along the parade's course. For example, at the sand box, have children build a sandcastle with wet sand. At the slide, have children roll up a large ball five times. Be sure to incorporate water and physical play—both are developmentally appropriate.

sensory "stuff." For example, fill tire one with soupy sand and linking toys. Fill tire two with wooden blocks. Place cars and dump trucks in tire three. Offer a variety of play experiences at each tire. Old tractor tires can also be turned into stimulating play equipment. Clean the tires first. Paint them for flare. Look at the accompanying illustrations for additional tire play path ideas.

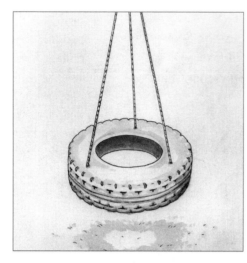

THREE-SEATED TIRE SWING—GREAT FOR SOCIAL INTERACTION AMONG PEERS

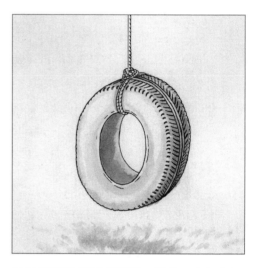

ONE-SEATED TIRE SWING—EXCELLENT FOR WORKING THE VESTIBULAR SENSE

OBSTACLE COURSE WITH TIRES LYING ON THE GROUND—WONDERFUL PHYSICAL PLAY

OBSTACLE COURSE WITH TIRES SPACED APART AND HALF BURIED IN THE GROUND— EASILY TRANSFORMED INTO GAME PLAY WITH BALLS

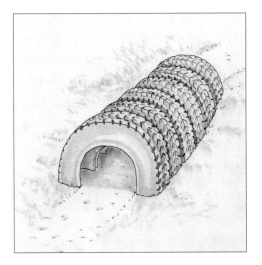

LONG TUNNEL OF TIRES BURIED HALFWAY
UNDERGROUND—PLENTY OF MOTOR PLAY
POSSIBILITIES ON TOP OF THE TIRES AND
INSIDE THE DARKENED TUNNEL

TIRE FILLED WITH SAND—A PERENNIAL
FAVORITE

When using tires in children's play, it is important to position the tires so they don't accumulate rainwater; standing water can be a source of mosquito breeding. It's also important to be aware that rubber tires contain volatile organic compounds (VOCs) and may also contain heavy metals. To prevent exposure to these hazards, be sure tires are not torn or crumbling.

OLD BARRELS: Large, clean plastic fifty-five gallon barrels can be turned into tunnels or situated for more entertaining play path possibilities. Children can also use clean barrels to roll around on a playground.

OLD ROWBOATS AND CANOES: Bury an old boat in the ground. Add creative boat play accessories, such as play fishing poles, nets, and tackle boxes full of rubber worms and other sensory things. Mount a wheel from an old stroller (preferably a large all-terrain wheel) as a steering wheel. Have a pirate adventure. Don't forget the telescope and a *walking* plank!

WINDOW WRITING: Let a child who roams decorate outside windows or inside mirrors with washable window markers. Make each window activity different, such as hand tracing at window one and portrait drawing at window two. Afterward, have the roaming child wash the windows with a huge, suds-filled sponge. On chilly days let children write messages on the icy windows with their fingers.

ACTIVITY WALLS: Visit Nasco online at www.eNasco.com to view a Sensory Stimulation Activity Center and a Wall-Mounted Kindertracker for a feel for activity walls. Then use pocket charts or sturdy Velcro to bring free-standing, interactive wall stations to life along a play path. Play a textured-shape matching game. Be creative using the seven senses for activity walls. Think button pushing, rope twisting, yarn stringing, ring tossing, or cork screwing!

Write a Play Plan

Children who roam often benefit from a visual schedule—a scripted play plan—of their playtime. A schedule that allows flexibility for varied attention spans works best. With a child who roams, write up a play plan. Allow the child to ponder "this" or "that" choices. A play plan can simply be written on a large index card or created with a graphic computer program. I recommend that play plans have at least three options. An example follows.

JAMAL'S PLAY PLAN

1. Broom shuffle

2. Newspaper toss

3. The delivery wagon

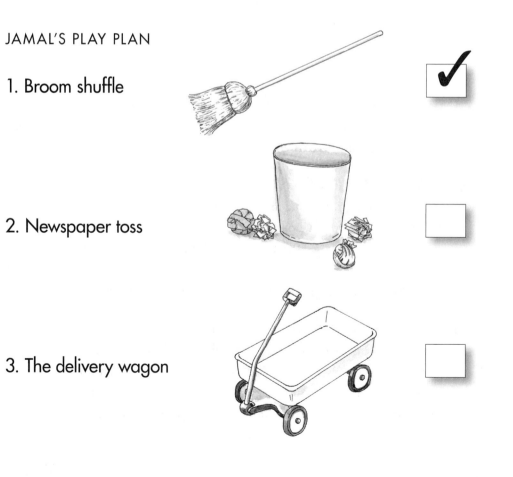

Listed below are explanations of Jamal's play plan:

1. Broom shuffle: Tape off a long, narrow shuffleboard lane in the classroom. Use colored mechanical tape to color code the lane. Lanes should be black, and the front lane line should be green. The end shuffle line should be red. Have the child stand at the front line of the lane and use a brawny push broom or kitchen broom to shuffle items, such as beanbags, hacky sacks, or heavier objects, such as secured and sturdy bags of rice, beans, or rocks, to the end shuffle line. Try a whisk broom or mop for variety.

2. Newspaper toss: Gather different textured papers, such as card stock, newspaper, and packing paper (see pages 39–40 for paper suggestions). Have the child who roams crumble individual pieces of paper and attempt to toss them into a pot, tub, or empty but clean trash can. Homemade duct tape balls or plastic bag balls are practical for this activity as well. For duct tape balls, crumble up wads of newspaper and wrap them in duct tape. For plastic bag balls, wad and knot up the bags. Individualize the sizes of the balls.

3. The delivery wagon: Tape a long line of duct tape across a classroom floor or outside on playground asphalt. Have the roaming child load large wooden blocks into a hefty wagon (see www.treeblocks.com for an assortment of wooden blocks). Have the child pull the wagon along the tapeline to a designated end point, unload and situate the blocks at a few different spots along the end point, and stack them into towers or pyramids.

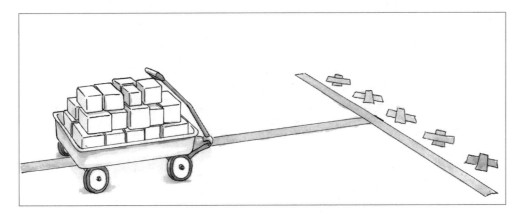

THE DELIVERY WAGON

Make an illustrated play plan for children. Allow them to check off each activity as it is completed.

An Individual Play Plan . . . for a Roaming Jamal

See page 21 for a discussion about the rationale of an individual play plan. Developing an individual play plan for a child who roams will assist in guiding you to support, include, and review his strengths, needs, and current observable and measurable performance in the areas of play concern. An individual play plan is meant to help you decide which strategies to use and how best to adapt or modify them to suit the child and ultimately lessen the play challenge. A sample individual play plan for roaming Jamal follows.

INDIVIDUAL PLAY PLAN

Child's name: *Jamal*

Age: *4 years old*

Play challenge or concern:

Jamal demonstrates no interest in peer play. Jamal's persistence in play is consistently observed at less than five minutes per task.

How does the play challenge affect involvement and progress in the general curriculum? For preschoolers and younger children, how does the play challenge affect involvement and progress in appropriate activities?

Jamal fails to attempt play or engage in play with his peers. He chooses to wander the classroom. Such behavior has left Jamal out of play

---

activities that would otherwise benefit his academic and social growth.

Additional present levels of performance:

Jamal continues to show delays in fine-motor, dexterity, and sensory skills in play activities. The delays promote frustration, which fuels unnecessary roaming.

Sample goal, benchmark, or short-term objectives:

Jamal will increase his play persistence from five to ten minutes with specific use of dexterity and fine-motor materials.

Possible methods of measurement for Jamal's goals:

- clinical observation of Jamal's performance (Adult observation of children is one of the most powerful assessment tools.)

- anecdotal notes about Jamal

- checklists

- rating scales

- products (samples of what Jamal produced)

- portfolios (items selected over time to show progress)

- audio and video tapes

- photographs

- journals

- informal interviews

- conversations

- conferences with parents or guardians

Sensory-integration strategies and activities attempted (briefly respond to each play activity):

The following activities were attempted with Jamal to increase his play persistence from five to ten minutes with specific use of dexterity and fine-motor materials.

Date: Oct 15 Activity: Play plan (found on pages 80–81)—Observation illustrated that Jamal was pleased with his visual play plan. He helped create the plan on a computer print shop program. We discussed each part of his play plan and how he would progress from one center to the next on colored tape after a timer went off. Jamal had to be reminded several times, however, to remain at the centers on his plan.

Date: Oct 18 Activity: Pumpkin play (found on page 66)—Observation illustrated that Jamal found pumpkin play frustrating. The slippery pumpkin seeds were difficult for him to manipulate.

Selection of activity and how it has benefited the child:

The visual play plan benefited Jamal in that he was pleased with his ability to choose his play activities. He wasn't able to check them all off, though, because he didn't remain at each center as discussed. The sticky insides of the pumpkin captured Jamal's attention for a while. He sorted the seeds with a peer and was eager to continue the activity when I suggested we wash and bake the seeds. Jamal began roaming, however, as we took turns washing the seeds at the sink.

Progress toward goals and objectives:

Jamal demonstrates minimal interest in peer play. His persistence in play remains consistent at six to seven minutes on task before roaming.

Has the child's goal been met?

Jamal has not increased his play persistence to ten minutes with specific use of dexterity and fine-motor materials.

Notes and comments on regression/progression:

Jamal continues to show delays in fine-motor, dexterity, and sensory skills in play activities. Although his skills continue to be delayed, the level of observable frustration Jamal experiences during playtime with peers has decreased. An array of other activity possibilities can be implemented with Jamal. Observation illustrates Jamal enjoys sensory tactile discs and stilt buckets. Incorporating these two activities into his daily routine would be beneficial in progressing his fine-motor skills and dexterity. Encouraging Jamal to join in peer sand play is also an option. He expresses interest in the dino dig sand toys. Such an activity would benefit him socially.

Wrapping Up

As you attempt to steer a roamer like Jamal to play, keep in mind that his sensory play menu should continually vary, not only in type but also in objective. Make sure to include reasoning activities to prompt cause-and-effect play and thinking, such as "When I play, I feel accepted and secure with my classmates. When I roam around and don't play, I feel left out and alone."

Offer play that prompts the clarification of pretend and fantasy. Offer play that prompts the release of bottled up emotions and energy. Offer play that promotes the use of social skills, such as taking turns and sharing, as well as language acquisition and communication skills. Ultimately, offer sensory strategies that steer a roaming child to "Come and play!"

Check out the following resources for additional sensory-integration play ideas for children who roam:

The Complete Book and CD Set of Rhymes, Songs, Poems, Fingerplays, and Chants by Jackie Silberg and Pam Schiller

Hands-On Nature: Information and Activities for Exploring the Environment with Children, edited by Jenepher Lingelbach and Lisa Purcell

Idea Box: Early Childhood Education and Activity Resources at www.theideabox.com

Nothing in the world can take the place of persistence.

—*Calvin Coolidge*

Securing the Anxious Child to Play

Anxiety or anxiousness is "a state of uneasiness and apprehension and fear resulting from the anticipation of a realistic or fantasized threatening event or situation, often impairing physical and psychological functioning," according to *Merriam-Webster's*. A simpler definition might be "the feeling that one's safety or well-being is threatened" (Dacey and Fiore 2000, 6). All children experience anxiety in one form or another, usually expressed as fear, worry, or excessive nervousness. As a play challenge, anxiety can be difficult to address depending on the degree to which a child may be experiencing it. For this reason, early intervention and journaling about patterns of anxious behavior are extremely important. This chapter focuses on anxiety not only as the dictionary defines it, but also in terms of a child's inner fear and worry. The two are often interchangeable in anxious children. Children suffering from anxiety need help when their anxiousness begins to interfere with their ability to thrive, play, and function on a daily basis. These children resemble anxious Anne in the example that follows.

Anxious Anne

One thing Anne finds most pleasurable is spending time with her father. Every day after school she waits by the window for him to arrive home from work—her nose pressed against the glass. Her father works at a car dealership as a mechanic. The job is physically demanding. Even at her young age, Anne is well aware of the toll the job takes on her father's body and moods. His day at work determines the direction of their evening time together, signaled to Anne by the stains on his work clothes. A heavily grease-stained shirt says, "I'm tired and want to be left alone. I've had a hard day. I'm worn out." A clean shirt, on the other hand, usually means he had a slow day; it says, "I finished my shift early without any complications. You can spend time with me. We'll share our day. You can sit on my lap, and we'll thumb wrestle each other." The five to ten seconds it takes for Anne to see the cleanliness of the shirt are nerve-racking to her. They are seconds filled with nervousness and worry. "Clean shirt or greasy shirt? Time playing with Daddy or walking on egg shells?" Unfortunately, anxiety over the shirt's cleanliness arises well before Anne's school day ends, commonly during afternoon playtime. The peculiar anxiety-producing event disturbs Anne's play patterns. Her creativity and focus as well as her ability to productively play all suffer.

Like Anne, children who appear anxious in play often play with apprehension, discomfort, and tension. Anxious children are often afraid to make eye contact with their peers during play. They engage in play activities timidly. An anxious child often enters into play as if afraid of it inflicting a sudden surprise. Although anxiety can be vented through various behaviors, if a child is displaying the following behaviors persistently, in a consistent pattern over an extended period of time, then an anxious play challenge may exist:

- The child freezes up, throws a tantrum, or becomes aggressive when asked to perform a play task.

- The child clings when separation from a parent or teacher is required for play. This is commonly referred to as separation anxiety and may happen at the start of each school day.

- The child obsessively fears unrealistic situations such as birds flying through open windows or closet monsters.

- The child insists on doing everything "just right" for approval.

- The child appears excessively nervous, irritated, or worried.

- The child only watches, suddenly withdraws, or begins to self-soothe through coping mechanisms such as nail picking, thumb sucking, hair twisting, or chewing.

A child's anxiety becomes problematic during play when she is unable to focus or remain at task long enough to learn from the activity. Luckily, "studies have shown that about 90 percent of all anxious children can be greatly helped by learning coping skills" (Dacey and Fiore 2000, 2). Journaling when and how children experience anxiety, taking detailed notes, is highly important. Doing so will help in discovering patterns or situational fears.

Reasons a Child May Be Anxious

Anxious symptoms in children are the result of a combination of factors, including biological, physiological, psychological, and social factors (Dacey and Fiore 2000, 8). A child may experience anxiety that is expressed in play due to a variety of reasons:

- divorcing parents

- chemical abuse in the family

- a family pet dies

- a dental visit is planned

- the child is a victim of abuse

- the child watches inappropriate or violent television shows

- the child begins attending a new school

Key Intervention Guidelines

The sensory-integration strategies on the following pages are useful in securing anxious children to play. The activities are respectful of the needs of nervous and worrisome children, and the strategies can be modified to remedy other play challenges or simplified or extended to meet the student's needs and interests.

Children who enter play anxiously will welcome the sensory richness of the strategies that can help them learn to play with ease.

Key intervention strategies for securing an anxious child to play are:

- Intervene as soon as you observe a consistent pattern of anxiety within a child's play.

- Support and respect an anxious child's feelings.

- Establish trust with an anxious child.

- Incorporate affection in an anxious child's daily routine.

- Make an anxious child's classroom safe and predictable, with a relaxed, noncompetitive, yet lively atmosphere.

- Offer a play menu that includes dramatic, physical, and outdoor play (time specifically spent with *nature,* not merely *outside the school building*).

- Incorporate an imaginative and revolving morning play center into an anxious child's schedule.

The coming pages present sensory-integration play strategies to secure an anxious child toward, in, or through play. Keep the following objectives in mind while considering the ideas.

1. Clearly look at the definition of anxiety as well as intervention strategies for an anxious child's behavior. Sometimes the answer to an anxiety problem is as plain as the nose on your face. Helping an anxious child may simply require

   - reassuring the child,

   - encouraging the child,

   - reassessing the child's background or new home setting,

   - speaking briefly with the child's parent or guardian about the child's regular sleeping and eating habits.

2. Refer back to the three principles of sensory integration on page 13. It is important to frequently revisit these three principles in order to reestablish the purpose of positioning a child to succeed within sensory-rich activities that are pleasurable and that shout, "Come and play!"

3. Rule out any basic health, vision, hearing, or learning disability possibilities that could be causing an anxiety-driven play challenge.

4. Unfortunately, anxiety in children can also be deeply engrained from previous or sudden trauma, abuse, or neglect, requiring more personalized or professional support. If this appears to be the case and the anxiety persists or increases in intensity over time (after several documented intervention attempts), hold a conference with the child's parent or guardian. Consultation with an outside community resource may be needed. Remember, early intervention is key!

5. As with all classroom, home, or center learning experiences, put safety, health, and age appropriateness at the forefront of all sensory-integration play exercises. Additionally—it's worth repeating—keep activities individualized, nonthreatening, and unforced.

Sensory-Integration Strategies to Secure an Anxious Child to Play

Sensory strategies to secure an anxious child to play follow. The activities provide a friendly avenue for anxious children to release feelings of frustration and ultimately learn to play naturally with age-appropriate peers while having lots of fun doing it! The strategies are fresh and easily modified.

Early Intervention

The early years are foundational for learning and playing. Make them count! If you observe a child with increasing anxious behaviors, intervene immediately by notifying the child's parents or guardians. Communicate openly and honestly with them about your observations and concerns. Ascertain their environmental and home perspective regarding the matter. It is imperative that parents and educators work together to help small children overcome debilitating anxiety. Building a partnership and intervention plan together is essential. To initiate a playful voice for an anxious child, try the ideas that follow and share them with the child's family.

CREATIVE CONVERSATION STARTERS: Anxious children often have difficulty vocalizing their feelings and frustrations. Try prompting playful conversations. Here are some suggestions:

- Initiate a sudden and short fingerplay or song, preferably one children have never heard.

- Say, "Nicholas, I have something in my pocket. Can you guess what it is?"

- Show the anxious child an interesting picture. Talk about it.

- Put on a fancy hat and ask, "Do you like my hat? Do you have a special play hat?"

- Ask the child if she'd like to pretend to ride a magic carpet. Let her steer the play ride.

- Change your voice. Make it crotchety or silly as you work or chat with an anxious child about choosing a play activity.

- Use a puppet or story mitt to initiate an activity. A funny face on the end of a tongue depressor stick is a simple and quick idea. Other puppet ideas include using socks, gloves, mittens, fingers, hands, spoons, bags, and Styrofoam balls with a stick inserted in the end.

ARTWORK: Art offers an especially beneficial way for children to vent emotions and anxious feelings. Put simply, art is a wonderful tool for self-expression and a catalyst for children to interact, share, look, listen, learn, and play! Use a variety of media and materials. Sit or sprawl out on the floor with an anxious child and creatively engage in art activities.

- Stamping stuff: Make colorful stamp collages with an anxious child. Little thumbs make perfect and quick stamping utensils. Offer a muffin tin full of sectioned out creative tidbits, such as small, snipped felt pieces, confetti, dried corn, or dry split peas to glue on stamp collages. Ready2Learn offers award-winning giant feeling stamps (Ready2Learn Giant Feelings Stamp Set; visit www .shoptheartstore.com/ready2learn.cfm). Stamps offer a great way for children to identify and put words to their emotions.

- Wall art: Every now and then let children "draw on the walls." Hang several layers of butcher paper or an old sheet. Offer a variety of utensils the child can use to freely decorate and draw. Turn to pages 32–33 for a list of wall-art tools. Let children draw on mirrors with dry erase markers. Wipe them clean with a tissue.

- Painting: Painting can be therapeutic for an anxious child. Use a variety of colors, textures, and brushes. Ready2Learn (www.readytwolearn.com) offers a wonderful set of painting texture tools that are perfectly sized for small hands. The set includes handles that hold a crinkly sponge, soft foam, foam strips, and chamois. An awesome paint substance to let an anxious child try is washable tempera paint mixed with sawdust and crushed chalk. Let him whip up a batch with an eggbeater. If paint materials drip, use cornstarch to thicken. Add extracts to the paint to give anxious children a sensory smell experience. Add peppermint to red paint, vanilla to white paint, lemon to yellow paint, and mint to green paint. Make sure to inform him that the scrumptious smelling stuff isn't edible. See pages 47–48 for more paintbrush and paint ideas. A sensory-integrated musical painting activity can be found on page 47.

Ms. Lilly
SI Play Tip

Some children may lack the coordination to hold their painting paper or artwork in place while working. Do something to stabilize the paper, which will help children focus on manipulating the utensils rather than wrestling the paper. Use masking tape or self-stick Velcro. Suction cups come in a variety of sizes and can hold toys down too.

JOURNALS: Journal writing can simultaneously act as an avenue to vent frustrations, express creativity, and hone writing skills. With an anxious child, write a letter to a friend or family member to express happy, anxious, or lonely feelings. Use a special pen, such as one with a fluffy feather. Offer a variety of creative materials, such as stickers, special stationery, and vibrating pens. Let her illustrate the letter as she wishes. This includes allowing doodles, scribbles, dots, and whatever the child puts down. Physically write the letter with the child either hand over hand or seated right next to her. While writing the letter, encourage conversation.

Make a feeling book out of a journal. Let the child acknowledge fears, frustrations, and other concerns through words and pictures in the book. Once the book is completed, read and discuss it together. For other terrific journal possibilities, visit Bare Books at www.barebooks.com.

QUILTING: Making quilts is a unique way to express one's emotions through the use of colors, fabric patterns, and steady stitching. Children often find quilting calming and relaxing. Simple quilting sets can be found at most discount stores.

With an anxious child, make a quilt from torn fabric strips tied into knots. Stitch a quilt with pattern pieces and patches. Talk about each patch. Make a noncloth quilt using a wallpaper sample book and a stapler or tape, with supervision, of course.

BALLOON RELEASE: Blow up different sized balloons with helium. After you have a big bouquet, take the balloons outside and release them with the children. Use this as a method to send off worries. Write anxious thoughts on paper, such as "Next week I have to go to the dentist. I don't like the dentist's office. It is scary and uncomfortable. My green balloon is my dentist worry." Model a balloon sendoff, and as you release the balloon, say, "Up, up, and away my worry goes!"

Sensory-integration enhancement ideas for balloon play follow:

- Papier-mâché balloons: Flour and water make a messy, wet substance children love! Tear old newspapers into strips, soak the strips in the papier-mâché mixture, and cover a balloon thoroughly with the wet strips. When the paper is dry, pop the balloon. Or let a child play in the mucky sensory mess using nonlatex gloves or brushes. A word of warning: This is a messy activity. Put several old sheets (or picnic tablecloths) on the floor.

- Balloon ball: Balloon ball is volleyball with a small balloon, minus the net. The rules are simple. Bounce the balloon back and forth in the air with the child, keeping it off the floor. For variety, use paddles or your feet.

- Stretch like balloons: Pretend to be big balloons with children. Stretch, breathe in air, and pretend to inflate. Then pretend to deflate as you "whoosh" air out. Other stretching ideas include moving like a flimsy paper doll. Stretch out, then stiffen, and move like a robot. Sneak like a playful kitten, and then stretch out again. Add music. Get creative!

- Balloon wraps: This activity is similar to papier-mâché balloons. It's a "lighter" version, so to speak. Use cornstarch and string or yarn. Simply coat a blown-up balloon with cornstarch and water. Then wrap the balloon in string while continuing to coat it with wet cornstarch. When dry, prick the balloon.

- Balloon stories: Make water balloons of all colors and sizes. Let children create characters out of them with permanent markers. Together, tell stories with the balloon people.

READ BOOKS: Many books that prompt discussions of emotions and situations that unfold in a child's life are available. Through books, anxious children (detached and rejected children as well) can learn to cope, relate, connect, appreciate, empathize, and understand their emotions, as well as those of others. Picture books are especially beneficial for younger, nonverbal children who are experiencing difficult inner situations. Add storytelling aprons (www.lakeshorelearning.com) and hand puppets to visually enhance stories. Use creative movement to bring parts of stories to life. For example, have children move their hands like caterpillars or shake them like rustling leaves. Legs can "bicycle" in the air or arms flap like a bird. Several literature choices that follow focus directly on feelings and difficult issues. Book reviews are available online.

Feelings

The Grouchy Ladybug by Eric Carle
Even If I Did Something Awful by Barbara Shook Hazen
I Was So Mad by Mercer Mayer
Don't Call Me Names! by Joanna Cole
That Bothered Kate by Sally Noll

Separation Issues

Will I Have a Friend? by Miriam Cohen
Going to Day Care by Fred Rogers
Lost and Found by Kathryn Hitte

Sibling Rivalry

The New Baby by Fred Rogers
The Quarreling Book by Charlotte Zolotow
This Room Is Mine by Betty Ren Wright

Divorce

Where Is Daddy? The Story of a Divorce by Beth Goff
Dinosaurs Divorce: A Guide for Changing Families by Laurene Krasny Brown and Marc Brown
I Don't Want to Talk About It by Jeanie Franz Ransom

Disabilities

I Have a Sister—My Sister Is Deaf by Jeanne Whitehouse Peterson

We'll Paint the Octopus Red by Stephanie Stuve-Bodeen (Down syndrome)

Looking After Louis by Lesley Ely (Autism)

Death

The Dead Bird by Margaret Wise Brown

Badger's Parting Gifts by Susan Varley (the death of a friend)

Saying Goodbye to Daddy by Judith Vigna

Adoption

The Really Real Family by Helen Doss

I Love You Like Crazy Cakes by Rose Lewis

A Mother for Choco by Keiko Kasza

Support and Respect a Child's Anxious Feelings

Like adults, children can't begin to understand their anxious feelings until they are properly brought to their attention, explained, and the cause rooted out. Until the child experiences repeated comfort in the area in which she is experiencing anxiety, the chances of managing the anxiety appropriately are slim. Don't pressure an anxious child to explain or understand why she is feeling what she is feeling. Be aware that your thinking the child is making a mountain out of a molehill doesn't make the anxious issues any less real, or make them disappear for that matter. Strategies that aim to support and respect an anxious child's feelings, with the goal of ultimately securing her to play, follow.

- Use circle time to "survey the scene." Circle time can be an effective time to access an anxious child's morning disposition. The observational time may give you a heads-up as to whether you may have to dig into your bag of tricks or tweak your lesson plans to accommodate an anxious child's morning mood.

- Speak in affirmations. Regular, sincere, positive affirmations are terrific for validating a child's true sense of self and worth. Affirm an anxious child daily.

- Respect preferences. If a child has obvious objections to touching certain play materials or playing in particular areas due to past experiences, respect the preference until progress is shown. Be ready with alternative activities or resources.

- Comfort a child who is distressed with coping mechanisms that cater directly to his interests and background. In short, lock into what the child enjoys and is familiar with. For example, while working on the Indian Reservation in New Mexico, I helped my students with special needs make fry bread dough. The making of the dough was my means of initiating conversation and helping them focus. It was their avenue to enjoying an afternoon snack.

- Practice positive verbal phrases when redirecting or guiding behavior and feelings. For example, "Terri, we use blocks for building," instead of, "Terri, don't bang blocks!"

- Allow an anxious child to bring a security object, such as a stuffed animal, to playtime. This is especially important after a traumatic event.

- Send an anxious child a cheerful letter or postcard in the mail expressing how happy and proud you are to have her in class.

Establish Trust with an Anxious Child

As an educator or child care provider, you have monumental power to shape a child's view not only of his play and learning but also of the world and how he chooses to maneuver through it. When you establish trust with an anxious child, you are creating a relational bond with limitless cognitive, emotional, and social guiding potential. Trust can be established in a variety of ways:

- Listen closely to an anxious child. Get down at her eye level and make direct eye contact.

- Take the time to know an anxious child and read her learning and frustration "cues."

- Respect an anxious child's strengths and weaknesses.

- Use reminders with kindness.

- Mean what you say and say what you mean.

- Model a positive attitude and perspective during an anxious child's difficult times.

- Give regular, positive verbal assurance (and tone does matter). Instead of "Don't run!" use "Please walk." Keep it positive.

- Constantly strive to understand the meaning behind an anxious child's behavior.

- Celebrate an anxious child's progress. Praise improvement!

- Follow through with promises made to an anxious child. If you promise a child a turn "later," make sure "later" happens.

- Respond quickly and consistently to an anxious child's needs.

- Be present regularly for an anxious child (not a habitually absent teacher).

Ms. Lilly
SI Play Tip

A child's emotional fitness is as important as his physical fitness. "Muscle it up" with daily affection, affirmation, and individual attention, which can be shown in the following ways:

- tousle a child's hair
- smile at a child
- pat a child's back or shoulder
- use special hand signs (a high five or secret handshake)
- give a hearty hug
- nod your head
- show a thumbs-up
- squeeze a shoulder gently
- wink
- laugh cheerfully with a child

Incorporate Affection into an Anxious Child's Daily Routine

Years ago I taught swimming lessons to preschoolers. One of the first lessons I learned in the required prerequisite CPR course was to stop and survey the accident scene—take everything in before reacting. Do the same when incorporating affection into an anxious child's daily routine. Some children thrive when given continual attention and affection. Others do not easily welcome them. Closely consider an anxious child's background when planning a menu of daily affection to alleviate anxiety. Regardless of any classroom situation, be mindful and respectful of a child's ability to offer and receive affection.

Several sensory-integrated ideas to incorporate affection into an anxious child's daily routine follow.

TELL SILLY STORIES. Take turns adding to tall tales, such as "Once upon a time . . ." Switch back and forth until the story is complete. Add creative body movements and props to enhance silly stories.

READ A BOOK TOGETHER. If children are reading, take time to sit one on one with each of them and listen to them read orally. With those who aren't reading, engage in interactive reading. Choose an age-appropriate book for the child (be sure it's one that will fit the child's attention span). Read the book ahead of time so that you can easily interact with the child about the story while you're reading it. Do so on a big comfy couch or in a pair of situated chairs. Extend book reading to a big refrigerator box with pillows inside as a private reading corner for an anxious child.

USE A SMALL CLASSROOM BULLETIN BOARD. As a special weekly display of a student's work, have the child bring in pictures, ribbons, or awards for accomplishments. Post super work. Post improved work.

HAVE LUNCH WITH THE CHILDREN. To involve parents, every now and then make it a "Lunch with Your Child Day." After eating, present a slide show of the students at work. Children love to see themselves in action.

GIVE A SMALL SURPRISE GIFT. With a small gift, attach a meaningful tag, such as "Suzanne, you've been a great helper this week." Give one to each child in the class if need be. Ideas include a piece of candy creatively wrapped, a mini coloring book, a seashell, or a jumbo jack set. Remember to consider age appropriateness.

HAVE A MARCHING PARADE. Let children make signs that express themselves. "My name is LeAnn. I like apples and popcorn. I have a brother named Sam." Parade around the school or center with the signs.

Make the Classroom Safe and Predictable

A child's play environment is where he develops cognitively, emotionally, socially, and physically. Although a perfect classroom environment doesn't exist, for anxious children one that is predictable, relaxed, and encouraging of noncompetitive interaction can work wonders! Regardless of the play challenge, a play or classroom environment shouldn't continually coddle a child who struggles. It should confront and test his limits, preferably using creativity and the child's learning preferences. Shoot to create a classroom environment where the child's play challenge isn't continually threatened. This can be achieved

Ms. Lilly
SI Play Tip

In a weekly or monthly newsletter, tell parents to turn lunchtime into an extra special treat using "lunchbox affection!"

• Pack specially shaped sandwiches using cookie cutters (big metal cookie cutters work best for bread slices).

• Using food coloring, make a heart on the child's sandwich.

• Wrap sandwiches in colored cellophane wrap.

• Use ribbon or heart stickers to decorate sandwich bags.

• Use thinly sliced banana or pumpkin bread to make a sandwich sweeter.

• Write a special message or put a lipstick kiss on the napkin you pack. Save napkins from restaurants, parties, and places visited and put them in lunches for variety.

• Pack a few Tootsie Rolls with a note attached, saying, "Hey Tootsie—you're on a roll!"

• Pack lunch in a brown paper decorated bag. Use a hot glue gun to attach colorful pom-poms, or hole punch a design and lace yarn throughout the bag.

Get creative. Write (and voice) "I love you" as much as possible too.

effectively for an anxious child by making the classroom safe, with a predictable schedule and a comfortable, upbeat, and noncompetitive setting. Listed are strategies for creating such an atmosphere.

- Always encourage effort. Never compare one child's work to another's. Be specific and use effective encouragement when praising a child's effort.

- When a child doesn't complete a task successfully, always start with what the child did right followed by what she has yet to master.

- Never pressure, belittle, or force an anxious child to participate or reluctantly share his feelings.

- Create an enthusiastic morning greeting and farewell ritual for an anxious child who struggles to part from a parent or guardian.

- Allow time for a morning presentation of the day's events. Create and post a visual "one task at a time" schedule. Verbally go over the schedule with the child daily, possibly first thing in the morning or during morning circle time. The schedule should be posted in the same spot each day.

- Model the schedule. Help an anxious child follow and listen to directions by modeling appropriate technique, behavior, and application of the schedule.

- Keep the schedule as routine and predictable as possible. Anxious children thrive in regular routines.

- Clearly define classroom procedures. An anxious child shouldn't worry if she *is* or *is not* doing something correctly.

- Incorporate regular movement breaks into an anxious child's schedule. Regular, creative physical movement is beneficial for all children, especially children experiencing anxiety or inner turmoil. Something as simple as standing and doing ten shoulder shrugs or counting twenty claps and hops will boost a child's energy level. Music to accompany fidget breaks is always encouraged.

- Close each day creatively. Make the child feel cared for and welcomed back. Give a high five or a vibrant, "Good job, Alfred!"

Ms. Lilly
SI Play Tip

Accelerate learning and encourage a quieter classroom for an anxious child with a WhisperPhone. The WhisperPhone (visit www.whisperphone .com) is a hands-free, acoustical voice-feedback headset that enables children to focus and hear themselves ten times more clearly as they learn to read, spell, focus, or process language. The Toobaloo (see http:// toobaloo.com) is a similar option also available online.

Offer a Play Menu That Includes Dramatic, Physical, and Outdoor Play

Playing with peers in an outdoor setting supports sensory-integrated, hands-on learning. Dramatic play and physical play offer opportunities for children to learn a variety of skills, including sharing, taking turns, and learning to compromise. When the three types of play are creatively combined, anxious children with play challenges benefit tremendously.

DRAMATIC PLAY

Dramatic play is much more than children dressing up in snazzy costumes and pretending to be community workers or role-playing a tea party for two. Dramatic play is a wonderful way for anxious children to express themselves and their emotions. A creative dramatic play area is a highly useful tool for observing anxious children. You can gain tremendous insight watching their play. Watch for these developing skills in the dramatic play area:

- literacy and communication skills

- social skills

- healthy pretend play

- responsibility (somebody has to clean up!)

- role-playing appropriately

- sharing and taking turns

Along with an assortment of flashy costumes, make a big box of shoes available in a dramatic play center. Add clogs, ballet shoes, tap shoes, galoshes, and any others you think a child might find appealing. Toss in accessories like magical hats, capes, hand mirrors, scarves, boas, briefcases, suitcases, hand puppets, toy stethoscopes, handheld massagers, and homemade butterfly wings made from gauzy nylon. Offer a variety of insect, bug, and animal costumes. Additional dramatic play ideas can be found on page 65.

PHYSICAL PLAY

Regular, vigorous physical play releases endorphins in a child's body that aid mental, emotional, and social development. Physical play involves flexibility, muscular strength, muscular endurance, and cardiovascular endurance. Physical play releases bottled up aggression and emotional energy. Experience has demonstrated that inactive children with a very sedentary lifestyle are not as mentally alert as their peers who engage in regular physical play and exercise. The bottom line is children simply grow, think, sleep, and focus better when they exert their systems daily through physical activity. Here's a phrase to help you remember the essentials for offering physical play to children: Children require *practice* at a *variety* of physical play *choices* that can be *simply demonstrated*. Here's that phrase broken down:

- Make sure children have ample opportunities to *practice* new physical skills and games.

- Offer a *variety* of physical play activities. Do you like to do the same thing over and over?

- Remember that children enjoy *choices*. Offer several physical play stations or games. Balance both structured and nonstructured play choices for children.

- Don't overcomplicate physical play activities with drawn-out, difficult directions. Keep activities in developmental "stage and age context." In other words, keep directions *simple*.

- Always model or *demonstrate* the steps ("how-to") for physical play games, regardless of how simple they are. Use as many senses as possible in the demonstration. Children will retain and respond to this more positively.

Here are several creative strategies for incorporating physical play into an anxious child's day.

OFFER A POGO STICK: Pogo sticks are novel toys. Children gravitate to them. Visit www.gifts.com for a Zoingo Boingo pogo stick, or www.backtobasicstoys.com for the Foam Maverick pogo stick and the Wooden Retro pogo stick. Also beneficial are Tippy Spots Balance Boards as well as Wobble and Rocker Boards, available from Ideal Fitness at www.shapeup-shop.com. Balance boards offer a challenging balancing act for beginners. Most reverse for more rigorous rocking action for the more advanced user.

PLAY BROOMSTICK LIMBO: This is a game children can play with minimal guidance. It is a great game to teach taking turns. Broomstick limbo is simple: Have two children hold a broom at both ends. Ask the other students to form a line in front of the broom to begin the game. Encourage students to walk, roll, or crawl under the broomstick as it is lowered turn by turn. Add music for more limbo fun.

HULA WITH HOOPS: Play hula hoop in the traditional manner— making the hoop twirl round and round by swinging your hips—or by laying several hoops on the floor and having children hop into and jump out of them. Alternate directions and movements. Have the children hop on one foot or with their hands in the air. Instruct them to pretend to be big jumping kangaroos or small hopping bunnies. Get creative. Visit Nasco at www.eNasco.com/earlylearning for additional large-motor physical gear, including hoop jumpers and ankle ball hops. Either one provides a fast and challenging aerobic activity that is helpful in developing upper and lower body strength.

USE BALLS: Pump up physical play with a variety of unique bouncing balls. Incorporate simple games with the following sensory balls, available from Ideal Fitness at www.shapeupshop.com, or at most discount and fitness stores:

- jumbo foam dice
- rhino skin foam balls
- giant globe balls
- giant exercise balls
- beach balls
- oversized cage balls
- giant mega balls (these are colossal!)
- reaction balls (balls with an unpredictable bounce)

All are fabulous for physical play and for improving eye-hand coordination. Basketballs and tetherballs are other options.

PLAY PANTOMIMING GAMES: Teach children to pantomime a story with exaggerated body movements. Have them pantomime a rigid robot, slinky snake, jumbo jet, sharp crayon, big butterfly, or gelatin. Have them wiggle and jiggle! Use props for even more fun.

Try this pantomiming exercise for "receiving a gift":

Ms. Lilly
SI Play Tip

A Giant Rocking Top (www.eNasco .com) can help develop a child's overall physical coordination. The child sits inside the huge top and rocks from side to side or spins in it. The top is an excellent vestibular sensory toy for indoor and outdoor play.

- Receive the gift and pantomime a surprised face. Cup your hand over your mouth.

- Marvel at the gift. Hold it close to your chest. Sway back and forth.

- Pretend to tear open the gift. Exaggerate paper flying everywhere!

- Discover the gift. Pantomime with gestures that the gift is awesome.

- Put the gift on a shelf. Dust off a shelf. Vigorously push things aside for the new gift.

Other pantomime ideas are playing tug-of-war; trying to open a window; opening a stuck jar; *really* enjoying a bowl full of yummy, cold ice cream; and walking like an elephant.

USE HOP BALLS AND HOPPING SACKS (POTATO SACKS): These are original physical play ideas. Children don't even know they are getting a healthy workout when they use big bouncers like hop balls and potato sacks. Have races on the playground. Large kangaroo balls can be used to increase body strength and balance.

TRY RAKING: Rake fall leaves into a big pile. Jump in. Lie down. Make "leaf" angels. Have children smell the leaves. Have children crunch them in their hands and between their fingertips.

TRY WASHING: Let an anxious child wash the classroom windows with a tub of soapy water and an oversized sponge. Let him dry them with a fluffy terry cloth towel.

MAKE STILTS: Make lightweight stilts out of tin cans for children to walk around on. Try sock skating on smooth floors (paper plates are also workable.) Stomp Walker Stilts are available online from Extex at www.extextoys.com.

PLAY CATCH: Use Sticky Splat Balls or Mini Water Ball Yo-Yos from Oriental Trading Company at www.orientaltrading.com for playing catch.

RIDE AND JUMP: Let children ride around on jumbo scooter boards (available at www.mansionathletics.com) or jump

Ms. Lilly
SI Play Tip

Big wagons and two-seated trikes encourage cooperative play and social interaction between children. If funds are scarce, a two-seated tricycle is often a more practical purchase than a regular tricycle.

with an exercise skip rope with lights and music (visit www
.atafa.com).

Here are just a few simpler physical play games—the possibilities really are endless! A word of caution: please always make sure there is plenty of room for a child's physical play activity.

- Play Twister or musical chairs.

- Play freeze tag, chase, or have races—"I'll race you to the fence and back!"

- Play Red Rover, Red Rover.

- Do the Hokey Pokey.

- Play tug-of-war.

- Play Red Light, Green Light.

- Crab walk or wheelbarrow walk.

- Engage in egg and spoon races.

- Use small balls to play cup catching. Throw the ball in the air and attempt to catch it in a cup.

- Blow bubbles. Have children chase and pop bubbles.

- Make tricycles available to ride. Offer ones with backseats for riders—a great workout for the pedaler!

- Put out a box of colorful juggling scarves for children to enjoy.

- Hang safe equipment for children to climb and swing from. Cargo nets work well.

- Play Hot Potato (see page 49) or Leap Frog.

- Try a game of "Mother, May I?" or Duck, Duck, Goose.

- Use or put up a basketball hoop for regular games of "h-o-r-s-e."

- Let older children enjoy a game of dodge ball.

Develop and explore a variety of creative and locomotor body movements that an anxious child can use throughout the day as well. Don't limit the activities to indoors. Venture outside on grass, in sand, gravel, puddles, leaf piles, dirt—and even mud! Here are some suggestions for creative body movements and locomotor movements.

Creative Body Movements

- Bend and bounce to "Head, Shoulders, Knees, and Toes."

- Shuffle your feet and arms back and forth as if cross-country skiing.

- Climb an inside climbing ladder. Put a big bell at the top to ring.

- Dance, scoot, shake, shuffle, slide, and sway to an aerobic tune! Add musical props (see pages 36–37).

- Hop, skip, or jump for a game of hopscotch. All you need for a quick outside game is a small rock and a piece of sidewalk chalk. If short on chalk, a stick for drawing a game in the dirt will do. Pump up the physical movement by having a child who is anxious jump on one leg while clapping. Get creative.

- Gallop and rock back and forth like a rocking horse to music. Add energetic arm movements.

- Roll back and forth on the floor. Or lie down on the floor with a child, touching feet. Try to roll across the floor without disconnecting your feet.

- Clap, wave, and stretch your hands to the sky.

- Draw pictures in the air with your chin or head. Clap your feet.

- Do aerobic movements, such as touching your elbows to your knees or your shoulders to your ears.

- Snap your fingers to a rhythmic rhyme. Add exaggerated marching or stomping steps. Add colorful ribbons and streamers.

Locomotor Movements

- Walk slowly with your eyes closed.

- Walk heavily like an elephant, swaying from side to side.

- Walk low with your toes pointed in.

- Walk barefoot with your toes pointed out.

- Walk backward, sideways, or diagonally.

- Walk on your heels or tiptoes.

- Walk using big steps or short steps.

- Stomp with knees high and out.

- Skate lazily.

- Walk on your heels in the sand.

OUTDOOR PLAY—TIME WITH NATURE

"Children between the ages of birth and six are sensorial explorers; they take in knowledge best through their senses. They gain better understanding when they involve themselves in activities that bring them into *direct* contact with the natural world" (Humphryes 2000, 16). A significant amount of research identifies a strong and positive correlation between the amount of time children spend in nature and their overall physical, mental, and emotional health. Here is some research to prove the point:

1. Children with nature nearby their homes are more resistant to stress; have lower incidence of behavioral disorders, anxiety, and depression; and have a measure of self-worth. The greater the amount of nature exposure, the greater are the benefits (Wells and Evans 2003).

2. Children who play regularly in natural environments show more advanced large-motor fitness, including coordination, balance, and agility, and they are sick less often (Grahn et al. 1997; Fjørtoft 2001).

3. Children who play in nature together have more positive feelings about each other (Moore 1996).

4. Natural environments stimulate social interaction between children (Moore 1986; Bixler, Floyd, and Hammutt 2002).

With regard to books about outdoor play, I find myself continually recommending two to parents and educators. One is Richard Louv's *Last Child in the Woods: Saving Our Children from Nature-Deficit Disorder* (2005, 54). Louv's "nature" remedies and opinions are pivotal, bold, and groundbreaking:

> Children need nature for the healthy development of their senses, and, therefore, for learning and creativity. This need is revealed in two ways: by an examination of what happens to the senses of the young when they lose connection with nature, and by witnessing the sensory magic that occurs when young people—even those beyond childhood—are exposed to even the smallest direct experience of a natural setting.

The other book I recommend is *Natural Playscapes: Creating Outdoor Play Environments for the Soul* by Rusty Keeler. In his book, Keeler takes readers above and beyond outdoor play experiences and activities. From towering sunflower-made mazes to natural soundscapes of wind chimes and metallic, wood, bamboo, and other natural noises, he presents awesome outdoor sensory projects. He even includes literal step-by-step nature playscape blueprints!

Sensory-integration strategies to connect an anxious child to playtime with nature follow.

MAKE AN OUTDOOR NATURE NOOK: Take advantage of outside seasonal changes when creating this area. For example, set the nook up as the leaves are changing colors. With the children, observe, discuss, and log the weather and nature changes surounding the nook.

To create the nook, beautifully situate a canopy under a big tree. Hang netting or gauzy curtains for a gazebo effect. String leaves, bells, and flowers around the nook area. Place log stumps or crates inside to sit on. Fill a box or two with interesting instuments. Here are some ideas:

- an auto harp
- a zither
- a shakere (gourd rattle)
- a small keyboard
- a child-size guitar
- homemade coconut cymbals
- a variety of kazoos or whizzers
- recorders
- snake charmers (www.shalincraft.com)
- bamboo flutes
- an assortment of handbells
- small bongo drums
- a child-size toy xylophone
- homemade rattlers and shakers
- musical bells and balls wrapped in suede or velour

Additionally, offer a tape recorder with a microphone and headphones. Make a tape of nature sounds. Record a

Ms. Lilly
SI Play Tip

Use flowers, bulbs, and cornstalks to create outside mazes for children to frolic, run, and dodge in and out of. For details, refer to *Natural Playscapes: Creating Outdoor Play Environments for the Soul* by Rusty Keeler.

thunderstorm, windstorm, and rainstorm or birds chirping, nighttime crickets cheeping, and night owls whooing. I suggest tapes, not CDs. They are easier for children to manipulate.

Whether you situate a tent, tepee, tarp, big box, or canopy outdoors, the following items inside or out can enhance a child's experience in nature:

- binoculars

- birdbath

- bird feeder

- birdhouse

- wind chime

- wind sock

"Natural" items left lying around a nature nook are tremendous learning tools. A jar of sap, a mysterious-looking seed or rock, an oyster shell, a prickly blowfish, a small seahorse, a rattling gourd, an amethyst or other crystallized quartz, or a moss covered rock can propel imaginative play. Use small cable spools as tables and display the exploration items. Plants enhance outdoor play areas. Attract butterflies by planting hollyhocks, asters, and parsley plants. Plant marigolds, sage, mint, and sweet pea plants to add color, texture, and scent to nature play nooks. Grow a cherry tomato tree; sweet corn; or a small herb, flower, or vegetable garden in an outside play area. Lock into all possible curriculum concepts with sensory integration and nature.

Ms. Lilly
SI Play Tip

To "catch" spiderwebs, sprinke a vacant one with baby powder. Put a thick piece of construction paper behind it and spray with hairspray. Take it back to class—or to your nature nook—to study!

MAKE A MUD MURAL: Hang an old sheet on the side of a building or lay it on the ground. Make a messy mud mural with a variety of textured mud. Whip up a batch of mud in an old gallon paint bucket and make it:

- thick and clumpy

- chunky with rolled balls of clay (meatballs!)

- soupy (mud mixed with pebbles, dry leaves, bark chunks, grass blades, hay strands, and a few shakes of sand as salt)

Give children paintbrushes of all sizes and let them splat the sheet with mud. This is messy and sensory stimulating.

With leftover mud, make puddles for children to muck around in. Let them put on oversized galoshes. Make plungers (specifically for puddle play) available. Again, this is messy and fabulously sensory integrated! See pages 34–36 for additional nature play ideas.

USE PICNIC TABLES FOR OUTDOOR PLAY: Simply getting outside in nature has the potential to calm and relax even the most anxious child. Use outside picnic tables to hook an anxious child to the beauty of nature. Situate a picnic table below a tree or beside a flower bed. Set up a listening center on one. Use a picnic table for an outside center and rotate a variety of meaningful and individualized manipulatives in color-coded bins. Manipulatives naturally encourage problem solving, making the activity an academically sound investment. Shoot for manipulatives that actively require the use of both hands:

- pipe builders

- snap cubes

- pattern blocks

- plastic coins

- foam dice

- linking people (www.lakeshorelearning.com)

- star builders

- tangrams

- bristle builders (soft interlocking bristled blocks)

- magnetic gears with interchangeable and turntable pieces (gear puzzles are great too!)

- design builders

- nuts and bolts builders

- stretch and connect builders

- waffle builders (all of the above are available through www.lakeshorelearning.com)

- Magna-Tiles, award-winning 3-D magnetic building tiles (www.magnatiles.com)

- Connectagons, a best-selling toy with geometric shapes having eight slots each in five bright colors (www.hearthsong.com)

Ms. Lilly
SI Play Tip

While she is in the classroom, purposely seat an anxious child next to a window with a scenic view of nature, which can positively benefit her mood. Plant a garden spot with flowers that attract butterflies right outside your classroom window. Flowers that attract butterflies include zinnias, marigolds, asters, and hollyhocks. If the child isn't easily distracted, hang festive stars, green plants, or mobiles. If the classroom doesn't have a window, seat the child next to an aquarium or a tabletop water fountain.

- classic manipulatives like K'Nex, Legos, Lincoln Logs, and dominoes
- traditional board and card games like Hi Ho! Cherry-O, Don't Spill the Beans, Perfection, Trouble, Go Fish, Crazy Eights, and Old Maid

Incorporate an Imaginative and Revolving Morning Play Center

Some children experience anxiety when they arrive at school. Separating from their loved ones can be difficult. To help with separation anxiety, set up an inviting morning imagination center. The center should provoke play. It should radiate, "Hey you . . . Come and play!" Items in the morning imagination center should be kept fresh and regularly rotated, and the child should look forward to it because the objects included are novel and not normally found at home. The imagination center should help the anxious child start each day calmly and in a predictable sequence. Imagination center ideas follow.

TREE BLOCKS: Fill a toy box with alluring wooden tree blocks (www.treeblocks.com) and a variety of different sized dinosaurs, jungle trees, or simple discount store zoo animals. Make a net or gauzy gazebo entrance to the center. Use a rod to drape a colorful curtain around the area. Add fabric or prism blocks to keep the center fresh. Prism blocks are transparent building blocks that radiate color when light passes through them. Find them from Fat Brain Toys at www .fatbraintoys.com. Remember, you are attempting to continually captivate the anxious child.

CRAYON EXTRAVAGANZA: Set out an assortment of crayons for a child to use. Fat ones! Skinny ones! Glittery ones! Silver, gold, copper, and bronze ones! Prang's 96 Color Tuck Box has fabulous fluorescent colors! Try Chunk-O-Crayons (www .dickblick.com), big, solid multicolored crayon chunks with streaks and patches. Melt old crayons together in shaped muffin tins. A heart-shaped crayon can be irresistible. Make crayon clumps, or wrap four to five crayons together with masking tape. Offer a variety of paper with a crayon

Ms. Lilly
SI Play Tip
Crayons often break when children use hard and vigorous strokes. Crayons also break from children who love to hear the sound of a snapping crayon or enjoy peeling off its wrapper. Steer clear of strict crayon rules for children with play challenges. Focus on creativity. Broken crayons can be melted down and used for a variety of projects. Search the Internet for "Uses for broken crayons."

extravaganza. Drawing on sandpaper or cardboard is a unique experience. See pages 39–40 for additional paper possibilities. Set out several crayon sharpeners in different shapes and sizes. Let the child use crayon shavings to make fun designs. Simply rub the shavings on paper.

SUGAR CUBE ART: Set up a festive-looking tabletop with bowls of sugar cubes. Lay glitter glue sticks out for the child to erect a sugar house, igloo, or bridge. For more focused fine-motor skill practice, pour glue in a plastic bowl and have children use craft sticks to get the glue and use it to assemble their sugar cube art. Set out sugar cube art examples for the child to see.

MARBLE TOES: Place an assortment of marbles in a box. Let the child remove his shoes and socks and attempt to transfer the marbles from one box to another with his toes. Make the activity more challenging by having the child keep his socks on or put big fuzzy socks on. Put the marbles in stuff, such as sand, Styrofoam peanuts, or shredded paper. When using marbles, always keep age appropriateness in mind.

MAZES: Make a maze or tunnel from several different-sized boxes. Cut windows in the box sides. Toss sticky balls, carpet squares, nesting blocks, or other interesting manipulatives inside.

TINKERTOYS: Children enjoy taking things apart or just tinkering with things. Make several tinker items available in a corner or on a side table. Ramps with accompanying small cars and blocks are ideal. Children can attempt ramp experiments or bridge work. A simple juicer is a perfect tinker item. Have the child put the juicer together, juice a few oranges, take it apart, and clean it. This is a supervised "tinkering" activity, of course. Or, use the construction tinkering toy set that has been a favorite for generations—Tinkertoys.

Ms. Lilly
SI Play Tip

Sensory sand possibilities are vast. Jurassic Sand is great for children with allergies. Quicksand is clean quartz sand that only requires water to turn into crumbly sandstone. Sandtastik is white play sand ideal for indoor sand tables. Moon Sand is sand that molds into any shape imaginable. Space Sand is sand that never gets wet in water and is used in NASA Mars Exploration Classroom experiments.

Ms. Lilly
SI Play Tip

Magnetize fabric blocks by splitting their seams, inserting super-duty magnets, and then restitching. The blocks will be usable not only for stacking, but also for attaching. Set out a variety of magnetic wands and accompanying items.

Here are a few more imaginative center ideas. Make prop boxes for quick, imaginative, and revolving morning play center change-overs. For example, to expand on the tree block center, toss in a variety of new toy vehicles, such as cars, dump trucks, trains, helicopters, wagons, and tugboats. A set of old blueprints and scented markers for drawing block *building plans* can instantly enhance the center. Wrap a variety of cereal and cracker boxes in wrapping paper, then mix them in with the other center blocks for the children to play with. To jump-start interest at a Tinkertoy center, set out an assortment of old clocks and cameras. Display a marble run (marbles on a winding and connected tubular track) at the marble toes area. Prop boxes or suitcases are also fantastic for switching the theme of a dramatic play center within minutes:

- Office prop box: This box might include paper pads, staplers, hole punchers, file folders, pencils, pens, an old typewriter, and a vase with plastic flowers.

- Hospital prop box: Include a variety of interesting props, such as stethoscopes, smocks, bandages, gauze, slings, prescription pads, dolls (as patients), and lab coats.

- Dramatic clothing box: Rotate the clothes in your dramatic play center. Offer more than conventional community costumes. Include glitzy getups like sequin skirts, capes, tutus, and vibrant boas. Hit thrift stores for a dazzling diva wardrobe that will spread sparkling smiles. Toss in black velvet pants, zebra-striped dresses, loud bell-bottoms, chiffon scarves, groovy sunglasses, petite-sized pageant gowns, tiaras, sashes, and marabou boas. Get funky with dramatic center clothing. Hang pictures from a variety of eras, such as the Roaring Twenties or the '50s and '60s for children to view.

If you are short on space and time, use prop bags. Hang them in the corresponding centers. A bag of PVC pipes from a hardware store can enhance almost any activity or center. The piping can isolate a child's voice for a pretend phone call at a dramatic play center or serve as a tool for a sing-along with a recorded musical selection at a listening center. Story time can be complemented with a small prop bag containing animal ears, noses, whiskers, and paws. Sales after Halloween are perfect for gathering props.

An Individual Play Plan . . . for an Anxious Anne

See page 21 for a discussion about the rationale of an individual play plan. Developing an individual play plan for an anxious child will assist in guiding you to support, include, and review her strengths, needs, and current observable and measurable performance in the areas of play concern. An individual play plan is meant to help you decide which strategies to use and how best to adapt or modify them to suit the child and ultimately lessen the play challenge. A sample individual play plan for anxious Anne follows.

INDIVIDUAL PLAY PLAN

Child's name: Anne

Age: 4 years old

Play challenge or concern:

Anne clings vehemently to her mother at drop-off time. Anne cries insistently for twenty-five to thirty minutes after her mother leaves. This disrupts morning free-play time for her as well as for her classmates.

How does the play challenge affect involvement and progress in the general curriculum? For preschoolers and younger children, how does the play challenge affect involvement and progress in appropriate activities?

Anne loses valuable morning play, building of skills, and social time with peers.

Additional present levels of performance:

Anne does not attempt to enter a play area, initiate play, or interact with her peers for almost two hours into the school day.

Sample goal, benchmark, or short-term objectives:

Anne will respond to a play activity within fifteen minutes after morning drop-off time. Anne will be allowed to bring in a tactile object from home to help soothe her separation anxiety. She will be allowed to bring it with her to morning playtime.

Possible methods of measurement for Anne's goals:

- clinical observation of Anne's performance (Adult observation of children is one of the most powerful assessment tools.)
- anecdotal notes about Anne
- checklists
- rating scales
- products (samples of what Anne produced)
- portfolios (items selected over time to show progress)
- audio and video tapes
- photographs
- journals
- informal interviews
- conversations
- conferences with parents or guardians

Sensory-integration strategies and activities attempted (briefly respond to each play activity):

The following activities were attempted with Anne to redirect her to enter a play area, initiate play, or interact with her peers.

Date: Mar 4 Activity: Crayon extravaganza (found on pages 111—12) Observation illustrated that Anne enjoyed the crayon center. She used the chunky crayons for a while and then the heart-shaped crayons the class had melted together earlier in the week.

Date: Mar 8 Activity: Outdoor picnic table play (found on pages 110—11) Observation illustrated that Anne found the outdoor picnic table play area soothing. During playtime she went to the table and sat alone, linking Legos. She spoke briefly with a peer but then returned to her blocks. Anne did spend a lot of time looking around.

Selection of activity and how it has benefited the child:

Anne benefited from the morning media center crayon extravaganza, as observed by her willingness to share her work with peers. She giggled quite often. Anne brought in a small stuffed rabbit and set it next to her while she worked at the center. Although not willing to share her rabbit toy, she did discuss her coloring with peers, which was progress. The afternoon outdoor setting for the outdoor picnic table play seemed to calm Anne. She took to the stories on tape and upon returning to the classroom, didn't ask how long it would be until her mother arrived.

Progress toward goals and objectives:

Anne has shown minimal progress in her ability to respond to a play activity within fifteen minutes of morning drop-off. She continues to mope for twenty to twenty-five minutes after her mother's departure. Anne brings in a stuffed rabbit from home to help soothe her separation anxiety. It appears to help her relax, but she is very reluctant to share the toy.

Has the child's goal been met?

Anne's goals have not been met. Minimal progress has been shown.

Notes and comments on regression/progression:

Anne appears to enjoy art projects, as observed from her taking to the crayon center. Creative supplies will need to be continually rotated to capture her interest and take her mind off her mother's departure. Sparkly items appear to appeal to Anne. The rabbit toy she brings in hasn't caused any problems between her and the other children; she will continue to bring it in to soothe her. Suggestions for moving forward with Anne include interactive reading with books of interest and outdoor musical painting activities. She responds well to such creative opportunities.

Wrapping Up

As was true with dabbling Mia, whether you're a first-year teacher or a veteran of the field, you'll also encounter an anxious Anne. It's not a matter of *if,* only *when,* and to what degree she will present her issues to you. Will you be ready?

A child's play is about individual expression. Emotions unfold within it in creative ways. As an educator, produce an environment in which your students will feel supported, respected, and secure enough to share their feelings as they play and learn. The use of sensory-integration play strategies is the perfect means for observing such expressions and seeking out the underlying causes of any anxiety. Anxious children can thrive under such conditions and ultimately feel invited to "Come and play!"

Check out the following resources for additional sensory-integration play ideas for children who are anxious.

Freeing Your Child from Anxiety: Powerful, Practical Solutions to Overcome Your Child's Fears, Worries, and Phobias by Tamar E. Chansky

Monsters under the Bed and Other Childhood Fears: Helping Your Child Overcome Anxieties, Fears, and Phobias by Stephen W. Garber, Marianne Daniels Garber, and Robyn Freedman Spizman

A Practical Guide to Solving Preschool Behavior Problems by Eva Essa

Preschool Handbook (Bank Street's Complete Parent Guide) by Barbara Brenner

Sand and Water Play: Simple, Creative Activities for Young Children by Sherrie West and Amy Cox

Never, never,
never, never
give up.

—*Winston Churchill*

Connecting the Detached
Child to Play

How would you best define the word *detached*? *Merriam-Webster's* defines it as "standing by itself: separate, unconnected." A simpler definition might be "separate and unconnected." Although play is an important feature of young children's lives, play patterns and partners vary considerably from one child to the next (Luckey and Fabes 2005, 67). Some children enjoy being connected to a playgroup. Detached children, however, prefer solitary activities and often play alone. They are quiet, resist help, and at times seem invisible. This chapter focuses on the child with a detached play challenge—the child who appears to be in his own little world and consistently demonstrates little or no interest in interacting with age-appropriate peers; the child who struggles to make eye contact with other children and who refuses mutual play with other children; the child who resembles detached David in the example that follows.

Detached David

On most days, David enters the classroom quietly. He puts his backpack away unnoticed. He sits at his desk silently. During free playtime, David gravitates to the block center, where he begins erecting creative towers by himself. Classmates surround David, but he pays little attention to them. He doesn't say much. He doesn't ask for much help. David plays alone, and he enjoys his play this way. He prefers a world of solitary play. Although David is not being disruptive or causing any trouble, his continual reliance on solitary play is problematic. Children learn and develop by interacting with one another. David isn't experiencing regular play interactions with other age-appropriate peers. He is not ingesting the benefits of cooperative play. David is demonstrating a detached play challenge.

If a child is displaying the following behaviors persistently, in a consistent pattern over an extended period of time, a detached play challenge may exist.

- The child continually and obviously avoids interaction with other children throughout the school day.

- The child continually demonstrates a stoic and uncomfortable disposition when participation with other children is necessary.

- The child sends off a message of "I want to be left alone!"

- The child displays stagnant and less than age-appropriate social-interaction skills.

- The child seldom engages in conversation with peers.

- The child keeps mostly to herself, rarely joining others in play.

- The child hesitates to participate in group activities that require interaction, such as holding other children's hands or talking.

- The child consistently turns down play opportunities when approached by peers.

Reasons a Child May Be Detached from Play

Children may detach themselves from their peers for a variety of reasons:

- A child may detach from peer play due to fatigue, hunger, or irritation. Hunger and fatigue can significantly alter a child's behavior and performance in school. Combined hunger and exhaustion can easily run a child down. Think of it this way: as an adult, how many people do you want to be around when you're tired, your stomach is growling, or you're discontent with a situation at hand?

- A child may detach from peer play due to poor communication or social skills. Children who find social interactions tense and stressful often remove themselves from play and spend time alone (Luckey and Fabes 2005). Children with such difficulties need opportunities "to engage in positive social interactions during play and other experiences, such as sitting together at the snack table or sharing seats on the bus" (Petty 2009, 80). A child's background and individual preferences often determine interest in social situations, friends, and the manner in which communication is carried out.

- A child may become detached from peer play because he is able to have more control over his individual play environment than when immersed in play with others. "When alone, children do not have to answer to others and are freed from pressures to do what others want them to do" (Luckey and Fabes 2005, 69). This can especially be the case for children with many siblings. Regular solitary play is important to them because it may be the only time they have control over their play (Luckey and Fabes 2005).

- A child may detach from peer play due to a naturally shy temperament. A reserved personality quality may be driving the detachment. Shyness refers to feeling awkward or distressed when around people one is not familiar with. Most shy children are not likely to become immersed in solitary play. Rather, they spend their time watching their peers play without them (Luckey and Fabes 2005, 70). They desire entry but simply need guidance in gaining access and interacting within play. As an educator, never label a child *shy* or *withdrawn,* especially in the child's presence. Their shyness may be a stage or personality quirk quickly outgrown.

- A child may detach from peers because she is an only child and used to solitary play. Playing alone and not having to share toys and spaces may seem normal and most comfortable to *only* children. Depending on their family's makeup and culture, some children prefer playing independently due to family dynamics.

- A child may detach from peer play due to lack of encouragement or stimulation at home (a lack of experience). Children who spend a considerable amount of time alone playing video or computer games and watching excessive television may prefer to do such because they aren't encouraged to engage in meaningful play with peers or family members. These children are accustomed to and stimulated by electronic play experiences.

- A child may detach from peer play due to a lack of trust for authority figures. Trust is earned. Unfortunately, if the adults in a child's life repeatedly break fragile boundaries and promises, a child will learn not to trust authority figures. Keep your word, say what you mean, and don't make promises you can't or do not intend to keep. Children are intuitive and can easily recognize authenticity. They do not enjoy being lectured, nagged, criticized, or judged, none of which makes the child's detached play challenge any less real. If anything, it will strengthen it and break down walls of trust.

Key Intervention Guidelines

To connect a detached child to play, it is important to express and model how worthwhile and fun play is! Lock into a world of creativity combined with the seven senses of sensory integration. When connecting the child to play, model progression through the play activity, preferably in guided steps or a sequencing of skills. This is when journaling is especially helpful, as is looking closely at a child's individual PLEAS C ME information. Journal in detailed notes about when and how intensely the child is detached. Doing so will help you discover patterns or uncover root causes.

Key intervention strategies for connecting the detached child to play follow:

- Play with a child who is detached. Model how playing with others is worthwhile and fun!

- Pair a detached child with a verbally and socially strong child.

- Communicate and work closely with a detached child's family.

- Focus on a detached child's social and play strengths. Build off them.

- Encourage, model, and coach prosocial behavior skills for a child who is detached.

The coming pages present strategies to connect a detached child toward, in, or through play. Keep the following objectives in mind while wading through the ideas:

1. Clearly look at the definition of detachment as well as intervention strategies for a detached child's behavior. Sometimes the answer to a detachment problem is readily remedied. Helping a detached child may simply require the following:

   - prodding the child with a variety of sensory materials

   - encouraging the child to explore new and different materials

   - reassessing the child's background and defining what is missing or not functioning appropriately

   - speaking briefly with the child's parent or guardian about the child's regular home play, sleep, and nutrition habits

2. Refer back to the three principles of sensory integration on page 13. It is important to frequently revisit the three principles of sensory integration to reestablish the purpose of positioning a child to succeed within sensory-rich activities that are pleasurable and that shout, "Come and play!"

3. Rule out any basic health, vision, hearing, or learning disability possibilities that could be causing a detached play challenge.

4. If a child's detachment from peers persists or increases in intensity over time (after several documented intervention

attempts), hold a conference with the child's parent or guardian. Consultation with an outside community resource may be needed. Remember, early intervention is key!

5. As with all classroom, home, or center learning experiences, put safety, health, and age appropriateness at the forefront of all sensory-integration play exercises. Additionally, keep activities individualized, nonthreatening, and unforced.

Sensory-Integration Strategies to Connect a Detached Child to Play

The coming pages provide a variety of ideas and exercises to connect a detached child to play. The activities are imaginative and hands on. They can be simplified or extended for student need and interest. A detached child will successfully respond to the strategies if continually encouraged to always do his best.

Play with a Detached Child

"During the preschool years, social competence begins to emerge and stabilize" (Petty 2009, 82). As an educator, you have tremendous influence on this area of development, which is just as important as the ABCs and 123s! Your body language, attitude, and enthusiasm in the classroom are powerful tools for directing detached children to play, as well as guiding their social skills. Lead a detached child to peer play by engaging in fervent play with her. Sit parallel with the child and participate in daily play activities. Guide and support the child's play efforts and patterns. Encourage the child to listen and talk as much as possible. When the child does interact, stretch out the conversation. Model how playing with others is worthwhile and fun. Continue to motivate the child with encouraging words. Draw the child into play with others by discussing and leading the child into simultaneous play interests. "Wow! Johnny loves to build big towers just like you do, David. Let's build one together. Just the three of us."

Use the strategies listed below to play and interact with a child who is detached. As you decide which exercises to use, keep in mind that presentation is everything. If you present a project or play space beautifully and enthusiastically, a detached child is likely to respond to it in the same way. While guiding and supporting play with the sensory strategies, continually be on the lookout for ways to enhance the child's interests and nurture further involvement. Finally, chatter with the child throughout your playtime together. Discuss a variety of topics.

MAKE A RAINSTICK TOGETHER: Rainsticks, traditional or home-made versions, are great projects for detached children. The sticks produce a calming, rainlike sound as they are turned from end to end, and children are intrigued by the sound and its mysterious source. Instructions for making the instruments are available at www.makeandtakes.com/rumblin-rainsticks. Guide the child as she works to create one. The project is sure to generate many questions and cheerful conversations between you and the child (Lamm et al. 2006, 22).

CREATE A PEACEFUL PLAY PLACE TOGETHER: "One of the most effective additions to the environment is a designated 'peace place,' a quiet, out-of-the-way spot" (Lamm et al. 2006, 24) where a detached child (or any child) can choose to go to play with a peer or to seek refuge when frustrated. The premise of the "peace place" is to allow a detached child a less stressful place to play. (A peace place is also ideal for anxious and rejected children.) Create and stock the area with the child while explaining its purpose: "Michael, you can come hang out here if you get frustrated or overwhelmed." Lay out big, comfy pillows and rugs. Hang unbreakable mirrors and engaging posters. Make sensory materials, such as playdough, available. Toss in a few musical instruments, such as the rainstick you made together! Don't forget to add books. A quick list of selected prosocial books for children follows:

The Way I Feel by Janan Cain
Today I Feel Silly and Other Moods That Make My Day by Jamie Lee Curtis
The Rainbow Fish by Marcus Pfister

PLAN A MENU TOGETHER: Bring in newspaper grocery store ads, and with the child who is detached, make a grocery list. Highlight the ads. Cut them out. Use them to plan each

Ms. Lilly
SI Play Tip
When working with detached children (anxious and rejected children too), implement a nonthreatening activity before the play session to release the child of any lingering fear, worry, or anxiety. Sandbox or ball pit play followed by rocking, swinging, running, or brisk hall walking are excellent prior-to-play options.

of your favorite meals. Clip coupons of the food items you'll need. Tally the cost of the items with an electronic cash register. Children often get a kick out of realistic registers with functioning calculators, beeping and flashing scanners, and pop-up sounding credit card readers. Visit Constructive Playthings at www.constplay.com for reasonable options.

MAKE A CLASS PICTURE TRAIN: Let the child take digital pictures of his fellow classmates. With the child, label the photos with his classmates' names and post a picture train of them on the wall. Display photos of classmates sharing and engaging in other prosocial acts (Petty 2009, 81). Let the child post the pictures on each of his classmates' cubbies (with their help). Allow the child who is detached to assist in making handprints of his classmates in plaster of paris. Guide the detached child to take on a leadership role with the project by mixing the plaster and setting his classmates' hands.

ERECT A FOREST: Using walls and partitions as backdrops, brown construction paper and empty wrapping paper rolls can become trees in a play forest. Cover the cardboard tube in brown construction paper and use it as a tree trunk. Using the wall as canvas, children can attach felt leaves or papier-mâché apples to the tree. Display a connecting fence with cut and painted cardboard. Lay down carpet squares in the forest for children to sit on. Get creative! In the forest, make available several play crates of musical props, books, blocks, and other interesting items. While in the forest with a child, follow his lead for play. Maybe erect a tree as in *Chicka Chicka Boom Boom* by Bill Martin Jr. and John Archambault. Add letters, as in the story, in papier-mâché. You also may want to try erecting a forest around the "peace place"—see page 125.

SPROUT SEEDS: Bring in small pots and potting soil and work together with the child to plant small flowers, herbs, or vegetables. Radishes and carrots are simple and easily transferred outdoors. Introduce the child to a spade, hand rake, watering can, and gloves. Discuss their uses. While sprouting seeds, encourage and prompt conversation with the detached child.

ACT OUT WORDS: With a child, act out words, phrases, and emotions without saying a word. Use facial expressions and gestures to express words and phrases like "Wow!" "I'm sorry," "Hello," and "See you later," for example, and to express emotions like embarrassment, silliness, guilt, happiness, fear, or pride. Or make up secret codes to send messages with musical instruments, such as small drums or rhythm sticks. For instance, make up a rhythm to represent "Keep up the good work" or "Only ten minutes until lunch."

PLAY PASS THE PICKLE: Pass the Pickle is similar to Hot Potato. With a child who is detached and a few other children, pass around a "pickle" or Koosh or Nerf ball to a variety of tunes. Or make a squishy ball to toss around as the pickle by filling two balloons, one inside the other, with flour or sand. A stuffed sock is usable too. Let one child control the music. Whoever is caught with the pickle in hand when the music stops is pickled out of the game! The last one with the pickle wins! If using a sock, dampen or weight it down with sand (and secure tightly) for added sensory value.

Ms. Lilly
SI Play Tip

A creative game that generates lots of laughs and fine-motor, skill-building potential is Wok 'N' Roll. In the game, children race to pick up food with chopsticks from a wok and place it in their bowls as the wok shakes and rolls. See www.toys4minds.com. Tongs can also be used for this game.

Pair a Detached Child

Peer modeling of social skills within play is wonderful for detached children. Children observe and naturally learn from one another. They discreetly coach, suggest, and, at times, demand. Pair a detached child with a verbally and socially strong child. When a child who is detached is combined with a child who is verbally and socially strong, the two can greatly benefit one another. The perfect chum combination can make all the difference in play direction and duration. In this partnership, a detached child can experience productively modeled play, stimulation of social skills, and chances to interact and talk.

Children with strong language skills can openly express how they can add to a play activity. "Hey, Hadley, I have some stickers we can use!" In doing so, peers are more welcoming. Children who are detached are often not as skilled at such open and expressive entrance strategies. Detached children who have difficulty voicing that they want to enter play are more successful when a socially and verbally accomplished peer guides their participation. This is formally defined as guided participation, in which "an adult or a more competent peer provides just the right level and amount of support to help a younger, less capable learner acquire skills and knowledge" (Petty 2009, 81). Guided participation is a useful technique for building social skills with children who are detached.

Sensory-integration play strategies targeted for peer play follow. Periodically partitioning the play area for more socio-dramatic play between the two children is a good idea. Additional peer play strategies can be found on pages 45–49.

HAVE A PANCAKE PARTY: Prepare several stacks of pancakes. Pancakes four inches in diameter work best. Provide an assortment of cookie cutters—not those used for playdough play though. Let the play pair cut out patterns from the pancakes. Add a few drops of food coloring to milk to use for paint. Use clean, small paintbrushes to decorate the cutout cakes. Allow the children to share one or two pancakes as a snack. To enhance the activity, allow the children to assist in preparing the pancake batter with a whisk and in flipping the cakes, with supervision, on a portable electric grill. Or turn the pancake party into a creative bakery center. Prepare instant pudding, no-bake cookies, or other simple snacks and sandwiches.

MAKE DANDELION MANES: Have the children work together to pick a small bucket of dandelions and then count their flower collection and remove the stems. On a large sheet of card stock or construction paper, let them draw or paint a big lion's face and then glue the flowers to make a mane. Or make a dandelion chain by knotting or taping the flowers together. Children can also place the dandelions in a bowl of water and use chopsticks, large tweezers, or small tongs to pick them out one by one. Have them see who can gather the most dandelions in the least amount of time. A small fishnet is also usable for this activity. Pay attention to allergies. Artificial flowers are an acceptable replacement for dandelions.

ENGAGE IN CLOTHESLINE PLAY: Hang a sturdy clothesline inside or outside the classroom using a nylon rope or twine. Fill a bucket with colored plastic or wooden clothespins. Place the bucket next to a laundry basket full of a variety of old clothes, such as a set of denim overalls, a Mexican poncho, a petite-sized wedding gown, a silk tie, and an old poodle skirt. Let the children hang the clothes on the clothesline. Inform them the garments should connect one after the other on

Ms. Lilly
SI Play Tip

Are your students experiencing grasping problems? Cookie cutters can be easier for small children to grasp by drilling a hole through the handle and inserting a shower curtain ring. Try wrapping pipe insulation around large sandbox tools or dramatic play kitchen utensils. Stick markers in sponge curlers for a better grip. Stick pencils through small rubber balls. Glue graspable knobs—corks or empty thread spools—on puzzle pieces.

the line. Slightly dampen the clothes to add weight for extra physical muscle work. Offer the children an old washboard and tub of soapy water to scrub the clothes before hanging them to dry on the clothesline. Fill the washtub with colored suds or toss in clothing scraps, such as canvas, cotton, silk, polyester, vinyl, wool, nylon, and a preemie-sized diaper in the clothesline washtub. Use a variety of shapes, sizes, and colors. Have children sort them out into smaller containers. The different materials will spark questions and require muscle work to wring out.

HAVE A TREASURE HUNT: Make a map for a simple treasure hunt. Have the hunt take place inside the classroom or outside. Lock into the children's interests and learning styles when creating the map and identifying the items to be hunted.

PRESENT EACH OTHER: Have the pair of children take turns introducing each other as if on stage. Use a play microphone. Practice and model an overdramatized introduction with them (Kettman 2005, 51).

READ *I SPY* BOOKS: Let the children read *I Spy* or *Where's Waldo* books. The books naturally encourage conversation and participation. If you hear the children talking "off task," let it be. The verbal interaction is good for the child who is detached.

PASS OUT PAPERS TOGETHER: Let the children work together in passing back assignments to their classmates.

USE PEDAL CARS AND SCOOTERS: Large-motor equipment and movement is beneficial to children. It allows for the release of excess energy, or blowing off steam, as well as building of strength and dealing with sensory-integration issues (Curtis and Carter 2005, 37). Classic Radio Flyer versions of large-motor equipment promote children taking turns. Most have working hand brakes and clutches for honing motor skills. The Radio Flyer Inchworm Model 73S is a bouncing and bobbing hit with youngsters!

PLAY SIMPLE GAMES: Play Bingo or Lotto games and allow the child who is detached to announce the numbers. Dominoes

Ms. Lilly
SI Play Tip

Rocking chairs and beanbags are perfect for library centers or reading nooks. HowdaHug Chairs are perfect for recommended reading time. They are movement oriented and promote sensory awareness. Visit Nasco online at www.eNasco.com/earlylearning for more information.

are a simple and versatile game for peer play. Try a colored, jumbo foam set or traditional wooden pieces. Get creative and raise the symbols on dominoes. Glue colored cardboard cutouts, sandpaper, noodles, or split peas to them!

ALLOW SIMPLE WALKIE-TALKIES AND MEGAPHONES: Walkie-talkies and megaphones come in all shapes, sizes, and varieties. Simple sets can be used on a playground for top secret play or cheering. Make accompanying prop bags, with a few plastic badges, notepads, pencils, and compasses for the walkie-talkies. Add pom-poms to the megaphones.

SHOVEL SNOW: If it snows where you live, let children shovel snow with child-sized shovels briefly during the winter months. Fill spray bottles with colored water and allow them to write in or decorate snow before shoveling.

DO A PARTNER WALK: Have the child who is detached and a playmate work together as a team in this trust-building game. Blindfold one of the children. Have the other child walk the blindfolded child to other areas in the room. The blindfolded child should try to guess their location.

USE A TIRE SWING: A tire swing is a surefire bet for sparking conversation and smiles from children. It guarantees eye contact between the children as they twist and turn. See pages 78–79 for additional tire play ideas.

PLAY MUSICAL JARS: Fill several identical jars with colored water. Encourage the children to experiment with sounds made by striking the jars with a variety of sticks, spoons, or musical resonating bars. Have the detached child be in charge of emptying and refilling the jars for sound making. Gather jars and bottles with a variety of openings and let children experiment with different sounds by blowing on their tops.

SORT BEADS: Mix a variety of beads in a large tub filled with birdseed. Shoot for a colorful mixture with different-sized beads. Have the children sift and sort through the birdseed to find the beads. Then they can use the beads to string a necklace or bracelet using fine twine, yarn, or thread. To expand on the activity, wet the birdseed or add sand.

Ms. Lilly
SI Play Tip

When children begin squabbling during play, a puppet or stuffed animal can often act as a good distracting or redirecting mediator in sticky, yet easily resolvable, situations (Kettmann 2005, 57).

USE GEL BOARDS: Gel boards are similar to whiteboards and chalkboards, but the child writes with a magnet on a gel board and erases with his finger. Visit Imaginetics online at www.gelboard.com for options.

Communicate and Work Closely with a Detached Child's Family

Family involvement plays a major role in redirecting a detached child's unfriendly and often isolating behaviors. For progress to occur, parents or guardians and educators need to get and remain on the same page. Schedule a conference when you feel you are veering off in different directions. Here are ten strategies you can use to help family members assist their detached child to play in and out of the classroom:

1. Make it a point to thoroughly discuss with parents the setting of realistic goals for their child, and emphasize how important this is. Express that change takes time and consistency.

2. Encourage parents to praise their child's progress and efforts.

3. Promote that parents set up playdates with their child's fellow classmates.

4. Regularly share the child's successes with family members.

5. Discuss with parents the importance of encouraging their child to interact with other children in environments outside of school, such as at the park, in church, or when visiting relatives.

6. Send home prosocial, behavior-building books for parents to read with their child. Suggestions can be found on page 125.

7. Suggest to parents that they not refer to their child as shy or withdrawn, especially in front of the child.

8. Explain to parents that continually scolding or harshly punishing their child for detached behaviors can be detrimental.

9. Encourage parents to read up on their child's play challenge or attend community discussions and workshops about it. Offer a suggestion or two from your own educational background.

Help a detached child incorporate more outgoing behaviors by using a variety of modes for demonstrating skill acquisition. Converse with the child while doing the following activities:

- buttoning (display articles of clothing such as suspenders that fasten to pants or winter coats with oversized buttons that twist and turn)
- catching a variety of balls
- checking off a list of materials needed for a project
- clapping patterns or rhymes or doing a hand jive
- climbing on ropes, stairs, or ladders
- coloring or painting
- cutting a variety of shapes from materials of assorted textures and thicknesses
- gathering items dropped on the floor and sorting them
- lacing items and combining them to form a basket or stocking
- nailing at a woodworking center
- pointing out the location of items requested without physically moving
- rolling on mats and forming body letters such as a *C* or *S*
- sifting through sand or other materials to find hidden treasures
- tapping out a sequence or pattern
- throwing sensory balls or beanbags
- turning knobs, nuts and bolts, or lids (to open and close containers)
- tying ropes, laces, plastic twine, or leather or cloth strips

10. Offer parents sensory-integrated home play center ideas. Suggest they engage in the activities with their detached child to encourage conversation and discussion. A home woodworking play area is an excellent starting center. Woodworking promotes several developmentally appropriate skills, namely eye-hand coordination, physical play, and creativity. Encourage parents to supply items such as softwood, lightweight hammers with easy-to-grasp handles, a variety of sandpaper, thin nails with large heads, wood glue, and wood scraps. And, of course, supervision and age appropriateness at a woodworking center are always recommended.

Detached children will benefit from creative assessment tactics that spark conversation and interaction. Open dialogue with the child and family members is needed to address a detached play challenge and to make progress with growth and development.

Working with families is one of the most important aspects of being an effective child care professional or educator, yet it is an area where many have received little training. To educate children well, we must include their families as much as possible. Considering the vast definition of family and its cultural, economic, and religious makeup, the task can seem overwhelming. Where does one begin in a society of single-parent families, families of divorce, blended families, extended families, homeless families, migrant families, and gay and lesbian families (Christian 2006, 12)? Here are a few suggestions for communicating effectively with all types of families:

- Continue to express the importance of teamwork. "We are working together for your child's education."

- Use open-ended questions and comments. "How can I help you with Elise?"

- Speak with clarity and specifics in regard to the child's progress. "Chris is doing much better in asking for help to open his milk carton and snack items."

- Use who, what, when, and where to gather information. Refrain from using why, as it often put parents on the spot.

- Steer clear of educational jargon and acronyms, such as IEP (Individualized Education Program), AYP (Adequate Yearly Progress), and NCLB (No Child Left Behind).

- Use encouraging gestures. A bright smile when informing parents of their child's progress (or even a lack of progress) is a wonderful start.

- Break challenges into manageable pieces. "Let's focus on Sarah's participation in morning play activities first."

- Always remain positive. "I'm looking forward to seeing how well Bill does next week. He continues to improve."

- Provide reassurance. "Eric is such a wonderful and hardworking boy."

(Bennett 2006, 26)

An educational home visit can help you better understand a child who is detached. Here are some tips to use if you visit a child and family at home:

- Arrive and leave at the time agreed on.

- Learn the names of family members, which are not necessarily "Mr. and Mrs. Cross."

- Assure the family of confidentiality.

- Encourage conversation, suggestions, discussion, and feedback.

- Keep the focus on the child's strengths.

- Always thank the family for their time and the privilege to be of assistance.

Keep in mind when working with families that *all* families deserve to be valued and respected. Continue to work as a positive unit with the child's family; this will greatly affect the child's educational experience. Trust is also a necessary component of any relationship and takes time to establish, so be patient with families. They may have had prior negative experiences with school districts. And remember, families are different and face challenges. Some may deal with mental delays, addiction, illness, or illiteracy—all of which affect communication skills and the ability to compromise (Bennett 2006, 26).

Finally, use the questionnaire that follows to gather information about a child's family at the beginning of the school year or before a home visit. Send it to the family along with a letter that introduces the questions with a welcoming introduction and ends with a friendly closure.

Questionnaire

Part One

1. Would you like to share your family's culture with our class?

2. What language do you speak most to your child? In which language do you primarily read with your child?

3. What are your family interests?

4. What are regular hobbies your family engages in?

Part Two

5. What goals do you have as a family?

6. What special skills does your family have? Would you be willing to share them with our class?

7. What days of the week work best for your family for conferences or school events, such as a family night?

8. Is there anything extra special you would like to share about your family?

Focus on a Detached Child's Social and Play Strengths

In the educational setting, children learn and develop social skills. For children, prosocial skills competence comes with experience and maturation. Children, especially detached children, require guidance and modeling to encourage the development of prosocial skills inside and outside of the classroom. Keep in mind that much learning of social skills comes with practice (Eliason and Jenkins 2003, 155). For example, sharing toys and taking turns appropriately and regularly don't happen overnight. Meet the child at his starting skill point and work forward from there.

Some social skills you can encourage and practice with detached children follow. Be creative in implementing and encouraging these skills:

- Follow classroom, center, and playtime rules, such as taking turns and sharing.

- Cope with name calling, teasing, and other antisocial classroom behaviors.

- Practice manners, such as saying, "Thank you" and "Please."

- Use eye-to-eye contact with peers and teachers

- Smile!

- Be courteous, kind, and helpful.

- Show empathy and compassion.

- Gain attention in positive ways.

- Share compliments.

- Show tolerance.

- Learn that actions have consequences.

- Take care of personal possessions
    (Eliason and Jenkins 2003, 155)

As you review the skills above, keep in mind that children come in a variety of packages. Some children require constant attention. Others are moody, controlling, or temper-tantrum prone, testing your patience and devotion on a daily basis. Regardless of her temperament, focus on the child's strengths. Zero in on what the child is doing correctly. Ask yourself, "What do I want the child to continue doing?" not "What do I want the child to stop doing?" Stay solution oriented.

Use the following six prosocial, behavior-building questions to help in the process:

1. How often is the detached child kind to other classmates?

2. How often does the detached child help others?

3. How willing is the detached child to share?

4. How often does the detached child demonstrate positive body language?

5. How often does the detached child show compassion or empathy toward a classmate in need?

6. How often does the detached child cooperate and interact with other children?

After answering the questions, use the following sensory-integrated strategies to focus and build on the child's social behaviors. Modify them for the child's areas of need.

- Use interactive board games and toys to reinforce prosocial behaviors, such as taking turns, cooperating, and sharing.

Ms. Lilly
SI Point to Ponder

You can help detached (and rejected) children strengthen their social skills in several ways:

- Focus on cooperative play rather than solitary play.

- Use interactive group games, such as musical chairs, to encourage prosocial play.

- Set up the classroom environment to facilitate cooperative play.

- Incorporate age-appropriate books and reading activities to support, encourage, and enhance prosocial classroom behaviors.

- Encourage social interaction among all the children in the classroom, including those with special needs and those who are linguistically and culturally diverse, as well as developmentally typical children (Honig and Wittmer 1996, 62–65).

- Situate the classroom to encourage more cooperative play and less solitary play. Make it a point to provide a surplus of creative materials and supplies for all the children. Always create ample space and time for play activities. Meander about the classroom encouraging peer interaction.

- Incorporate prosocial, behavioral-building books during story time and daily reading activities. Focus on books that capture the detached child's interests. Emphasize books with repetitive phrases and rhyming words as well as beautiful illustrations. Here are some children's books that increase understanding of social behaviors, self, and others:

  Whistle for Willie by Ezra Jack Keats

  Whoever You Are by Mem Fox

  Smoky Night by Eve Bunting

  Bread, Bread, Bread by Ann Morris

  Friends in the Park by Rochelle Bunnett

  Two Good Friends by Judy Delton

- After reading the books, have children take turns sharing with a partner something they found intriguing or new in the stories. Or have them retell the story to each other using a felt and flannelboard, magic slate, or puppets. Add creative props, music, or movement to enhance book reading.

- Role-play positive social behaviors using skits. If a child who is detached is having a hard time using the right words to express himself around his peers during skit performances, put on a puppet show beforehand to welcome the child in and lighten the mood. Add cheerful music, such as a round of "If You're Happy and You Know It."

- Incorporate small community service projects into the curriculum:

  Pick up trash from the playground together.

  Plant flowers around the school together

  Work or read with other children

  Put together a simple food or clothing drive.

Ms. Lilly
SI Play Tip

Go nuts with literature in your classroom. Books are some of the best teachers. Read aloud to your students every day. Display new books regularly, especially beautifully illustrated ones. Encourage children (and parents) to share and trade books. The Franklin the Turtle series by Paulette Bourgeois is an excellent set to suggest for at-home use as well as to have shelved in the classroom library. Books in this series discuss issues parents may encounter on the home front:

- *Franklin Is Bossy:* Franklin learns his friends don't like it when he bosses them around.
- *Franklin Is Messy:* Franklin learns he must be responsible and clean up after himself.
- *Franklin in the Dark:* Franklin learns not to be afraid of the dark.
- *Franklin and the Thunderstorm:* Franklin learns to overcome his fear of thunderstorms.
- *Franklin Fibs:* Franklins learns the consequences of lying.

Encourage, Model, and Coach Social Skills for a Detached Child

Walk the walk you talk! Set a good example to encourage and coach progressing prosocial behavior skills for a detached child. For young children to learn proper social skills, proper social skills need to be modeled, valued, and promoted not only in the classroom with words and actions, but also in curriculum activities. Incorporate sensory-integrated activities to teach a child, especially a child who is detached, the following skills.

- Interact positively with peers, smiling and greeting other children, teachers, and parents by name. A simple social interaction game is to have children sit together in groups of two or three and ask them to think of things that come in twos, threes, fours, and fives. Have them draw, paint, or graph their findings. Use the creative drawing and painting utensils listed on pages 47–48.

- Be considerate. Have children practice situations, such as opening the classroom door for one another or helping each other put center toys away.

- Use kind words. Have children face one another and exchange compliments, such as, "I like your shirt. It's a nice color."

- Help others. Have children help each other clean out their desks or cubbies with fluffy terry cloth towels. Children should be encouraged to help each other with small classroom chores, such as straightening books or toys.

- Use manners. Have children stand face-to-face and hand each other small items. Inform them to communicate with "Please" and "Thank you," as well as by listening and looking others in the eye when being spoken to.

- Cooperate. Have children work in pairs to clean blocks and toys with soapy water at a classroom sink. One child washes the items. The other dries them.

- Share. Bring in a small snack and have children cut the treat in half and share it with another child. Healthy, nutritious, sensory snack suggestions include pineapple slices, orange or apple wedges, strawberries, pretzels, carrot sticks, cheese chunks, raisins, and cooked spaghetti strands. Always consider children's allergies when making food selections.

Ms. Lilly
SI Play Tip

Detached children who are given the opportunity to take on leadership roles during play are more likely to become active and eager participants. For example, allow a detached child to be Simon in a game of Simon Says. Do not exclude children from group leadership roles because of their play challenge.

Ms. Lilly
SI Point to Ponder

"Conflict resolution is a process involving cooperative negotiation to achieve mutually acceptable (win-win) solutions" (Dinwiddie 1994, 14). Engaging children in interactive social problem-solving activities that involve the discussion of their feelings and needs will teach the process of conflict resolution. Threatening, nagging, bribing, assigning time-outs, or ignoring behavioral situations will not teach conflict resolution and positive social skills (Dinwiddie 1994, 14).

• Take turns. Have a pair of children take turns pushing each other on an outside swing.

Singing is a developmentally appropriate practice and instantly heightens any skill or concept. Singing can help children with play challenges to strengthen their communication and social skills. A simple song can be transformed into a play activity that focuses on creative movement, art, drama, and dance. Sing vibrantly to encourage and enhance prosocial behavioral skills. Incorporate sign language.

Instruction is more effective when it is grounded in meaningful context (Katz and McClellan 1997). Several additional suggestions and strategies for teaching prosocial skills to children who are detached follow. The ideas for many of these activities can be found on the Web site of the Center on the Social and Emotional Foundations for Early Learning at www.vanderbilt.edu/csefel. On that site under Resources, click on Practical Strategies. The activities can be used for other play challenges as well.

MODELING WITH OR WITHOUT PUPPETS: Model the desired skill while explaining how to properly carry it out. Puppets are useful while modeling because they can allow for creative role-playing. For example, lay out an oversized puzzle, scattering all its pieces on the floor. Using a puppet, model how to ask for pieces and to work as a team, "Mr. Puppet [or make up a name], what do you think we should do if somebody grabs a puzzle piece out of our hands?"

USING PEER PARTNERS: Children can and will learn from one another. Prompt children to help and encourage each other in areas in which they need assistance. For example, "Sasha, could you help Susan practice standing nicely in line? I think the two of you can practice with one another while we wait to have our pictures taken."

USING PROMPTS: Verbal, visual, and physical prompts, such as voicing a transitioning warning, posting a schedule, or using a hand puppet, are useful and effective in teaching social skills. A verbal prompt may resemble the following example. Kyra has difficulty entering into play with her peers. She usually barges in and demands things. When you see Kyra ready

Ms. Lilly
SI Point to Ponder

How would you rate your students in the following five areas during play?

• Movement: Is the child a busy bee, a mover in continual motion? Is the child an easygoing, low-key kind of kid?

• Consistency: How does the child handle a structured and predictable day of play versus one of an opposite nature? Is the child unpredictable and spontaneous during play?

• Change: Does the child adjust to change easily or come unglued at the slightest modification of play plans?

• Attention span: How long can the child stay focused during play? Is the child easily distracted during play?

• Emotion: Is the child sensitive to particular issues during play? High-strung? Overall upbeat and positive?

Knowing a child's unique formula for playing will assist you in more proactively guiding his behavior and planning his play.

to make her socially unacceptable move, you might discreetly say, "Kyra, don't forget to ask your friends to play. I bet they will say yes if you ask nicely."

OFFERING CONTINUED PRAISE: When you witness a child properly performing social skills, immediately give praise and encouragement. For example, "Will, I saw you and Gretchen playing cards together. You were taking turns nicely. Good job!" Keep in mind that praise can be verbal or nonverbal. See pages 66–68 for additional information on the power of effective encouragement.

USING TEACHABLE MOMENTS: As an educator, take advantage of teachable moments to reinforce or encourage social skills. Here's an example. During snack time you are a few crackers short. Juan volunteers to share with his classmate. Use the moment to praise his choice and kindness. Follow up by allowing Juan to divide and share his crackers accordingly.

PLAYING GAMES: Games can teach several social skills, including problem solving, identifying feelings, being a friend, and even using manners.

An Individual Play Plan . . .
for a Detached David

See page 21 for a discussion about the rationale of an individual play plan. Developing an individual play plan for a detached child will assist in guiding you to support, include, and review his strengths, needs, and current observable and measurable performance in the areas of play concern. An individual play plan is meant to help you decide which strategies to use and how best to adapt or modify them to suit the child and ultimately lessen the play challenge. A sample individual play plan for detached David follows.

INDIVIDUAL PLAY PLAN

Child's name: David

Age: 5 years old

Play challenge or concern:

David struggles to interact consistently during playtime with his classmates. David struggles to make eye contact with classmates. David struggles to initiate or engage in peer conversation.

How does the play challenge affect involvement and progress in the general curriculum? For preschoolers and younger children, how does the play challenge affect involvement and progress in appropriate activities?

David fails to attempt or engage in cooperative play. He refuses to attempt or engage in play activities involving more than two children. This interferes with David's ability to participate in many class play activities. David is noticeably indifferent to peer play and interaction. This leads to David being left out of play activities that would otherwise benefit his academic and social growth.

Additional present levels of performance:

David continues to demonstrate delays in social and communication skills, such as asking for help when needed. Although not initiating play, David is showing improvement in remaining in the same area with his classmates during playtime. He isn't meandering off to private corners of the classroom as much.

Sample goal, benchmark, or short-term objectives:

David will demonstrate attentive listening skills to enhance relational peer social skills. David will increase participation in back and forth peer conversation. David will respond to peer conversation with eye contact. David will increase participation in classroom social play.

Possible methods of measurements for David's goals:

- clinical observation of David's performance (Adult observation of children is one of the most powerful assessment tools.)

- anecdotal notes about David

- checklists

- rating scales

- products (samples of what David produced)

- portfolios (items selected over time to show progress)

- audio and video tapes

- photographs

- journals

- informal interviews

- conversations

- conferences with parents or guardians

Sensory-integration strategies and activities attempted (briefly respond to each play activity):

The following activities were attempted with David, who struggles to initiate or engage in peer conversation, make eye contact, and interact consistently during playtime with his classmates.

Date: Sept 13 Activity: Sprout seeds (found on page 126)—Observation illustrated that David enjoyed sprouting seeds and working with the soil. David planted three kinds of herbs. He carried on a brief conversation with his peers about his grandma's flower garden. David continued to emphasize how his grandma didn't like cats to get in it. "Grandma gets mad when cats are in her garden."

Date: Sept 16 Activity: Pancake party (found on page 128)— Observation illustrated that David interacted well with his peers while preparing the pancake batter for the pancake party center. He asked to add cinnamon to the batter when it was his turn to whisk the mix. He verbally selected his cookie cutters and why he picked them but did so while looking down at the floor.

Selection of activity and how it has benefited the child:
The two activities benefited David largely in the area of social skills. He was eager to show peers his planted herbs and share his pancake cutouts. David continues to look down at the floor instead of at his peers' faces.

Progress toward goals and objectives:
David is progressing toward his goals in all areas except peer eye contact.

Has the child's goal been met?
David's goals have not all been met, but he is steadily progressing.

Notes and comments on his regression/progression:

David's listening skills for enhancing his relational peer social skills are improving, as are his back-and-forth peer conversations. David's eye contact with his peers continues to be weak. David talks to the floor. His participation in classroom social play is improving.

Wrapping Up

To connect a detached child to play, you can model, encourage, and facilitate lots of meaningful conversation and interaction in stimulating ways. Providing a nonthreatening "prior to play" experience may be needed at times to set the stage. Your encouraging words may be just what a detached child like David needs to join in sensory-integration play with his peers, such as "David, would you like to help Keesha build a block tower? Let's ask her together." Creative music, props, or parallel play may propel a detached child forward. Engaging in and stretching out interesting chitchat for as long as possible might also help to involve the child who is detached. Or try a focused floor activity with a puppet or two. Remember, keep a detached child's play natural, safe, and inviting, expressing gently, "Come and play. It's fun to spend time with your classmates."

Check out the following resources for additional sensory-integration play ideas for children who are detached.

An Activity-Based Approach to Developing Young Children's Social Emotional Competence by Jane Squires and Diane Bricker

Learning to Care: Classroom Activities for Social and Affective Development by Norma D. Feshbach and Seymour Feshbach

The Peaceful Classroom: 162 Easy Activities to Teach Preschoolers Compassion and Cooperation by Charles A. Smith

*Don't let what you
cannot do interfere
with what you can do.*

—*John Wooden*

Helping the Rejected
Child Play

Merriam-Webster's Collegiate Dictionary defines the verb
reject as "to refuse to accept, consider . . . or use." In
other words: to deny. One of the most painful scenes
a parent or educator can observe is a child being continually
rejected by his playmates. Social rejection for children is a play
challenge that requires immediate attention. Parents or guardians
and educators need to work together to accentuate and build off
of the child's strengths in order to improve the social weaknesses
fueling the play challenge. Children who are continually rejected
or denied play access by peers are not only at risk for social play
problems but also for academic problems. For children who have
been rejected by their peers, school can be uninviting, frustrating,
and lonely, lacking peer approval and connections to peer play.
This chapter focuses on children who are continually rejected by
their playmates. These children struggle to make friends and fail
to stay within the boundaries of sociable play. Rejected children
often exhibit behavior that is obnoxious, bossy, aggressive, unpredictable, or volatile. They have trouble reading obvious social
cues. These children resemble rejected Ricardo in the example
that follows.

Rejected Ricardo

Bilingual Ricardo is six years old. His English is weak, and his Spanish accent is thick. Classmates have difficulty understanding him most of the time. They laugh at him. Ricardo responds to their heckling by hitting them. During center time, Ricardo enjoys the dramatic play center. His teacher, Mrs. Warren, has supplied cultural connecting clothes for him, including a sombrero with a matching poncho. Ricardo loves wearing the brightly colored attire while playing house. He often becomes aggressive, pushing the other children when they won't play according to his cultural norms or when they laugh at the big hat. His hostile behavior has caused the other children to avoid him, not only during center time but also on the playground and at lunchtime. Unfortunately, Ricardo's behavior has led to his being rejected by his peers. This is a play challenge requiring immediate intervention.

A child who displays the following behaviors persistently, in a consistent pattern over an extended period of time, may be at risk for social rejection by peers.

- The child intimidates peers with aggressive behaviors, such as hitting, slapping, or name-calling.

- The child acts immaturely (with extreme silliness) or overexaggerates play.

- The child is often self-centered and not sensitive to the needs of others.

- The child moves haphazardly from one activity to the next.

- The child plays oddly; for example, she hits or throws dolls.

- The child has poor impulse control (a very short fuse).

- The child demonstrates language and communication delays, resulting in fits of frustration.

- The child expresses emotions inappropriately. Common examples include crying excessively in front of his peers; growling bizarrely when upset; or huffing, puffing, and stomping off when not given his way.

- The child may be rejected by peers simply because the other children do not want to share their play materials or space with the child.

Reasons a Child May Be Rejected by Peers

A child may be rejected by playmates for a variety of reasons:

- The child is unpredictable during play. Unpredictable children tend to be moody. Their ability to persist in play shifts quickly—either they give up easily or practice extreme stick-to-itiveness, leading to outbursts if interrupted. Unpredictable children tend to overact when excited (clapping and flailing wildly) or demonstrate intense sensitivity to otherwise small issues (crying and tattling). Both can easily disrupt play activities and cause a child to be rejected.

- The child fabricates tall tales or brags excessively. Even children do not enjoy being around a know-it-all or have-it-all. Constant bragging and exaggerating can cause peers to reject a child.

- The child tattles excessively. Although tattling is something all children do at one time or another, rejected children who have trouble relating to their peers often use tattling as a last resort approach to communication. It is a way for them to feel comforted during frustrating situations with their peers. Rejected children may also tattle excessively because they don't know the difference between a situation needing to be communicated to an adult ("Jill fell off the slide") and one that does not ("Billy is using too much glue").

- The child has poor social skills. A child who has been rejected by her peers may have poor social skills, such as not being able to appropriately share or take turns. Acquiring situational appropriate social skills is a process that takes time and guidance. Some children require more time, guidance, and encouragement for social interaction and cooperation skills to develop than others. Unfortunately, until mastered, children can be rejected for lacking such necessary skills.

- The child is bossy and controlling. Children do not like taking orders from their peers during play. Children who dictate play and its materials can be easily rejected by peers. Bossy or controlling children can quickly find themselves ignored when their strong-willed, aggressive personalities kick in. Many bossy children are searching for structure, while others simply do not know how to play cooperatively. Bossy children may have felt bossed around by other peers and are trying out the behavior on others.

- The child is neglected, unclean, or unkempt. Regardless of economic circumstances, as educators we need to help a child who has been rejected fulfill individual potential. Poverty and neglect in children's lives can disrupt their learning process, but it doesn't determine failure. Unfortunately, children can be cruel to their peers who are struggling in this area, with comments like "You smell!" or "Who gave you such a dorky haircut?" This can lead to a child being rejected or left out of play.

- The child exhibits cultural differences, speech delays, disabilities, or physical impairments. A child with a limp, scar, lisp, or tic, or a child who is confined to a wheelchair may be rejected because of other children's fears or confusion.

Key Intervention Guidelines

To help a rejected child overcome a play challenge, communicate and work closely with family members. Model prosocial skills using sensory activities. Children who risk rejection from peers benefit tremendously from a consistent, clear, and calm schedule. Buddy play is equally advantageous. Regardless of the play challenge, journaling is also helpful, as is looking closely at a child's individual PLEAS C ME information. Journal in detailed notes about peer interaction with a child who is risking rejection. Doing so will help you discover patterns or uncover root causes.

Key intervention strategies for helping the rejected child to play follow:

- Place a rejected child with a responsive, socially skilled playmate.

- Use drama and other creative activities to help a rejected child to play.

- Communicate and work closely with a rejected child's family.

- Focus on a rejected child's social and play strengths. Build off of them.

- Encourage, model, and teach prosocial behavior skills for a rejected child.

- Teach a rejected child to problem solve.

- Use the three *C*s: be *calm, clear,* and *consistent* with a rejected child.

The coming pages present strategies to help a rejected child toward, in, or through play. Keep the following objectives in mind while wading through the ideas.

1. Clearly look at the definition of and intervention strategies for a rejected child's behavior. Sometimes the answer to a child's rejection can be readily remedied. Helping a rejected child to play with peers may simply require the following:

   - redirecting the other children or the child who is being rejected

   - encouraging the child

   - reassessing the child's background

   - speaking briefly with the child's parent or guardian about the child's regular home play habits

   - speaking with the class about feelings and how they would feel if they were rejected or left out

2. Recall the three principles of sensory integration on page 13. It is important to frequently revisit the three principles of sensory integration to reestablish the purpose of positioning a child to succeed within sensory-rich activities that are pleasurable and that shout, "Come and play!"

3. Rule out any basic health, vision, hearing, or learning disability possibilities that could be causing a rejection play challenge.

4. If a child's rejection from peers increases in nature (after several documented intervention attempts), hold a conference with the child's parent or guardian. Consultation with an outside community resource may be needed. Remember, early intervention is key!

5. As with all classroom, home, or center learning experiences, put safety, health, and age appropriateness at the forefront of all activities. Additionally, keep activities individualized, non-threatening, and unforced.

Sensory-Integration Strategies to Connect a Rejected Child to Playmates

Children who are rejected often have difficulty following classroom rules and resort to disruptive behavior to gain attention during play. Children who risk rejection are disrespectful toward peers and lack skills for sharing play materials. Such behavior often forces them out of peer play. Sensory-integration strategies to connect a rejected child to playmates follow.

Ms. Lilly
SI Point to Ponder

Like tolerance, rejection is a learned behavior. Never allow a child to outrightly reject another in play without intervention. Keep mental notes on the children you pair together for sensory-integration play activities. You'll quickly discover how the individual learning styles of children feed off of each other positively.

Place a Rejected Child with a Responsive and Socially Skilled Playmate

Peer modeling of social skills within play is wonderful for rejected children. Children observe and naturally learn from one another. They discreetly coach, encourage, and at times demand each other's attention. When a rejected child is combined with a friendly and socially skilled playmate, the two dispositions can greatly benefit one another. A perfect chum combination can make all the difference in play direction and duration, ultimately producing positive play opportunities. When appropriately connected with a friendly and socially skilled playmate, a rejected child can productively experience play, stimulation of social skills, and chances to interact and talk.

Sensory-integration play strategies that are targeted for peer play follow. They promote prosocial behaviors like taking turns, sharing the responsibility of cleaning up, and helping each other along. When and where applicable, periodically partition the play area for more socio-dramatic play between the two children. Additional peer play strategies can be found on pages 127–31.

PLAY T-BALL OR OTHER COMMUNITY SPORTS: Encourage good sportsmanship and teamwork with a vigorous game of T-ball. Try a Big Bopper T-ball set, which increases a rejected child's chances of hitting success, so is perfect for building self-esteem. Encourage parents to sign their child up to play on a community organized T-ball or sports team.

DIRT PLAY: Seek permission from an administrator to dump small dirt mounds on your center or school playground for children to play in. Dirt is different from sand, as it is not granular and tends to stay very cool when shaded. Children will enjoy discovering and exploring dirt's texture as they dig into the mounds. Encourage deep hole digging with shovels and ice cream scoops, which is excellent physical muscle work. Allow children water access to fill the holes for homemade boating adventures. Set out several chunky trucks with scoops for dirt play. Bury plastic worms, bugs, twigs, acorns, small stones, lemon and orange peels, pinecones, and other little treasures to add to sensory exploration. Have children play buried treasure, in which one child buries a surprise and the other digs it up. Start a compost pile and turn the dirt mounds into healthy soil.

Children are naturally attracted to muddy, messy, and creative areas of play. Here are some additional ideas.

- A little clay play: Unlike dirt, sand, playdough, and mud, clay's texture is cool, malleable, and warms to the temperature of a child's hands (Rogers and Steffan 2009, 78). Clay smells like earth and can be easily stored by tying it up in a tablecloth.

- A digging hole: Children love to dig and dig deeply. Corner off a dirt area for purposeful digging. Bury objects beforehand. Supply small spades and shovels. Let them see if they can reach China!

- A moat: Start a small moat around a sectioned area of sand or dirt. Let children extend, deepen, and add water to it. Use twigs, branches, and other natural items to build bridges and dams. Supply plenty of digging utensils in all shapes and sizes.

- A dino dig: Turn a sandbox into a junior archaeological dig perfect for aspiring paleontologists. Use a variety of sand textures; see page 112 for ideas. Hide plastic bones and dinosaur skeletons in the sand. Offer excavation supplies, such as sturdy sieves and brushes for scooping and dusters for dusting off exciting prehistoric discoveries.

- A garden bed: Together with children, plant a variety of flowers to attract insects and emit wonderful fragrances.

Ms. Lilly
SI Point to Ponder

Rushing in to resolve a child's dilemmas during play is a true disservice. It robs her of valuable opportunities to develop vital conflict resolution skills, such as active listening, positive body language, and brainstorming solutions (Ramsey 2003, 104). Let the child work out minor frustrations in play as much and as long as possible before intervening. As a teacher or child care provider, you can do specific things to help children resolve their own conflicts and gain skills they will carry well into adulthood:

- Help them stay focused on the solution, not the problem.
- Help them see the effectiveness of negotiation.
- Empower them to be problem solvers.
- Hold regular class meetings where everyone gets a chance to speak.
- Encourage the use of props, such as puppets and books, to help guide children through the process of conflict resolution (Carlsson-Paige and Levin 1992, 9–12).

Flower beds offer fantastic sensory experiences for children to play directly with nature.

LOOFAH RUB: With a back-rubbing or loofah bath brush, have a pair of children "draw" on each other's backs. Encourage them to write silly words, decode them, and then erase with the brush. Encourage shape and picture back drawings.

BASKET SORT: Bring in an assortment of mismatched socks in a large laundry basket. Have children sort and match up the pairs. After all the pairs are matched and balled, let the children play "basket" ball. Place the laundry basket against a wall. Put down a circular masking tape line for children to stand behind and shoot the balled socks into the basket. Extend the activity by making sock puppets.

Other simple activities for a rejected child and a more socially skilled playmate to do together include sorting crayons and tossing out what's old; straightening a bookshelf; dusting tables with big feather dusters; sweeping the floor using a variety of brooms; or wiping tabletops with clean, wet rags or wet wipes.

Use Creative Arts and Drama to Help a Rejected Child Play

Children who are rejected often grapple with anger management and conflict resolution issues. At times, they also struggle with showing respect for self and others. To assist with such obstacles during play, use cooperative learning and group dynamic activities that involve creative art and drama.

Ms. Lilly
SI Play Tip

A wonderful sensory-filled musical experience for young children is the Neurosmith Jumbo Music Block. With it, children learn shapes through songs, exploration, and activities! Visit www.geniusbabies .com for more details.

PLAY BELLS: Provide two to three children with an assortment of bells of various types and sizes, such as jingle bells, handbells, tubular bells, resonator bells, and even cowbells. Encourage the children to experiment with the bells and talk about their different sounds. Prompt them to talk about which bell they find most appealing. Model how to handle the bells carefully and take turns ringing them. Ask the children to restate back to you the rules for bell play. To enhance the activity, you might bring in small instruments and bells from different cultures and produce a puppet show to share with the class.

MAKE MARACAS: Let children make maracas together. This activity is a great extension of the "play bells" activity above. Offer paper plates, empty plastic soda bottles, pie tins, and paper towel rolls. Provide "stuff" such as rice, sand, coins, marbles, and beans to fill the instruments. Help the children make up a march to share with their classmates. Have the children try to guess what's shaking inside individual maracas. Add to the activity a few tunes from *Songames for Sensory Integration* (audio cassette and booklet) by Lois Hickman and Bob Wiz.

MAKE BUDDY BOOKS: Have children draw or paint self-portraits on paper. Add a photograph to each child's masterpiece. Clearly write the child's name on the bottom of their page and bind all the children's pages together as a book to put in the library center.

MARSHMALLOW PLAY: Set out toothpicks and several bowls of a variety of marshmallows, including big, small, multicolored, coconut, and chocolate. Allow children to use the marshmallows and toothpicks to create animals. Children can also use the sticky side of contact paper to make 3-D creations with small marshmallows and glue.

MAKE MASKS: Mask making can become an extravagant dramatic art project with endless craft possibilities. It can also be kept simple with a few paper plates, scissors, and yarn. Take mask making to a suitable play level, depending on the child's individual needs. Use finished masks to role-play or perform short skits or plays to reinforce social skills. Enhance sensory-integration play by making edible masks out of baked tortillas. Use powdered sugar and food coloring as paint. For additional ideas, check out *101 Drama Games for Children: Fun and Learning with Acting and Make-Believe* by Paul Rooyackers.

MYSTERY BAG PLAY: Have children close their eyes or use a blindfold. Invite them to use only their sense of touch to identify objects that are hidden in a mystery bag. Items to discover may include craft feathers, fur pieces, dried coffee grounds, fruit chunks, or cereal pieces. You can tap into all of a child's senses with mystery bag play.

Ms. Lilly
SI Play Tip

One of the best classroom play areas to work on social skills is the dramatic play area. A creative dramatic play space or program can teach children to interact positively with their peers and learn to compromise. A large selection of hats in various shapes, sizes, and textures that symbolize a variety of characters and cultures is a must for a thriving dramatic play area. Incorporate hats, such as the following:
- a large chef's hat
- a real construction worker's hat
- a Western cowboy hat
- a colorful sombrero
- a jeweled crown
- a French beret
- a Southern belle bonnet

Creatively display the hats on a hat rack or on wall hooks.

Ms. Lilly
SI Play Tip

Dance is a wonderful expressive art for children who are rejected. Dance options are numerous, including ballet, tap, hip-hop, swing, ballroom, Irish, jazz, and country. Just get children up and movin' and groovin'! Add props like movement scarves and individualized costumes.

HAND PLAY: Have children put personality and life in their hands. Have them shake each other's hands together quickly or angrily. Make up crazy hand jives to funky music. Pretend to have nervous hands (shake them wildly), strong hands (clench them tightly), or magical hands (perform slow roller-coaster waves).

PEER MAKEOVERS: Let children use face paint to turn each other into creatures or princesses. Offer a box of costumes and props to enhance the makeovers.

PIED PIPER PLAY: Play instrumental or simple flute music. Instruct children to follow an appointed child leader and imitate his moves and actions. See page 106 for creative body movements to enhance Pied Piper play.

Communicate and Work Closely with a Rejected Child's Family

Family involvement plays a major role in redirecting a rejected child's social behaviors. Parents or guardians and educators need to get and remain on the same page for progress to occur. Schedule a conference when you feel you are veering off in different directions.

Listed below are ten strategies to help family members assist their rejected child to play.

1. Discuss with families the importance of setting realistic goals for their child who is play rejected. Express that change takes time and consistency. Communicate openly and plainly with parents and guardians.

2. Encourage families to praise their child's progress and efforts.

3. Promote that parents set up playdates with their child's fellow classmates.

4. Regularly share the child's successes with family members.

5. Discuss with parents the importance of encouraging their child to interact with other children in environments outside of school, such as at the park or when visiting relatives.

6. Send home prosocial, behavior-building books for families to read with their child. Suggestions can be found on page 136.

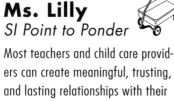

Ms. Lilly
SI Point to Ponder

Most teachers and child care providers can create meaningful, trusting, and lasting relationships with their students; it's creating the same kind of relationships with children's parents that can often be tricky. In her book *Parent-Friendly Early Learning: Tips and Strategies for Working Well with Families,* Julie Powers offers fundamental techniques for laying the groundwork for good partnerships with families. Visit Redleaf Press at www.redleafpress.org for details.

7. Suggest to families that they not label or refer to their child in negative terms, such as "bratty," "impossible," or "not like his siblings," especially in front of the child.

8. Explain to parents that continually scolding or harshly punishing their child for rejected behaviors can be detrimental. Emphasize progress, not perfection.

9. Encourage families to read up on their child's play challenge and any continued patterns of concern. Offer a suggestion or two from your own educational background.

10. Offer families sensory-integrated home play center ideas. Suggest they engage in the activities with their rejected child to encourage conversation, growth of social skills, and discussion on various prosocial subjects. A home card-making craft area makes an excellent center. With a supply of old greeting cards for cutting, gluing, pasting, coloring, and making utensils of all sorts (refer to pages 39–40 for ideas), and an assortment of glue (colored and glitter) and other craft supplies to use in creating new cards, families can enter into a variety of social conversations. Here are some examples of conversation starters:

    - When we hurt another child's feelings, we need to apologize, and we can do so in a variety of ways, such as . . .

    - When we want to wish somebody "good luck," "good job," or "good-bye," we can do so in these ways . . .

    - When we miss somebody, we can express that like this . . .

    - When we are sad, mad, or frustrated with somebody, we can respond in a variety of positive ways. For example, we can . . .

Focus on a Rejected Child's Social and Play Strengths

Children come in a variety of packages. Some children require constant attention. Others are moody, controlling, or temper-tantrum prone, testing your patience and devotion on a daily basis. Regardless of her temperament, focus on the child's strengths. Zero in on what the child is doing correctly. Instead

Ms. Lilly
SI Point to Ponder

Communication notebooks are an excellent tool for communicating daily with a child's parent or guardian. This notebook is a two-way journal stored in the child's backpack. It goes home nightly with teacher comments written inside regarding the child's school day. It returns the next day with any parental comments or concerns. Use the comments and observations as a tool to outline a child's parent-teacher conference.

Ms. Lilly
SI Play Tip

In a parent newsletter, suggest the following free or low-cost places and activities for families to engage with their children and create play memories:
- camping
- playgrounds
- picnics (indoors and outdoors)
- community events
- nature walks
- farms or petting zoos
- art galleries
- bike rides (Kettmann 2005, 328–29).

of asking, "What do I want the child to stop doing?" ask yourself, "What do I want the child to continue doing?" Stay solution oriented.

Use the following six prosocial, behavior-building questions to help in the process of redirecting a child who is at risk for peer rejection.

1. How often is the rejected child kind to other classmates?

2. How often does the rejected child help others?

3. How willing is the rejected child to share?

4. How often does the rejected child demonstrate positive body language?

5. How often does the rejected child show compassion or empathy toward a classmate in need?

6. How often does the rejected child cooperate and interact with other children?

After answering the questions, use the following sensory-integrated strategies to focus and build on the child's social behaviors. Modify them for the child's areas of need.

- Use interactive toys to reinforce prosocial behaviors, such as taking turns, cooperating, negotiating, and sharing.

- Situate the classroom to encourage more structured cooperative play. Studio-like spaces and quiet coves filled with creative block building materials promote peer play, whereas crowded or narrow rows of desks do not. Make it a point to provide a surplus of creative materials and supplies for all the children. Post visual procedures of play centers with accompanying rules for children who struggle with cooperative play. Always create ample space and time for play activities. Meander about the classroom encouraging proper peer interaction. Redirect poor play behaviors head on.

- Incorporate prosocial, behavioral-building books during story time and daily reading activities. Encourage choral reading of the books. Put them in the library center or have the child who is rejected read one of the books to a peer. Here are some children's books that increase understanding of social behaviors, manners, self, and others.

The Ant and the Elephant by Bill Peet
Clifford's Manners by Norman Bridwell

Me First by Helen Lester
The Little Engine That Could by Watty Piper
Horton Hatches the Egg by Dr. Seuss
Hands Are Not for Hitting by Martine Agassi
When Sophie Gets Angry—Really, Really Angry by Molly Bang

After reading the books, have children take turns sharing with a partner something they found intriguing or new in the stories. Or have them retell the story to each other using a felt and flannelboard, magic slate, or puppets. Add creative props, music, or movement to enhance book reading.

- Role-play positive social behaviors through short skits or dramatic performances. Use ideas from stories you have read. If a child who is rejected is having a hard time using the right words or actions to express himself around his peers during skit performances, put on a puppet show beforehand to welcome the child in and lighten the mood. Add cheerful music, such as a round of "If You're Happy and You Know It."

- Incorporate small community service projects into the curriculum:

  Pick up trash from the playground together.
  Plant flowers around the school together.
  Work or read with other children.
  Put together a simple food or clothing drive.

- Lead a child who's been rejected to take on a leadership role, under your supervision and guidance, of course.

Encourage, Model, and Teach Prosocial Behavior Skills for a Rejected Child

Children who have been rejected can display wild, woolly, and bully personalities. They can be intense and often struggle with the following social behaviors:

- poor table manners

- inappropriate language

- grabbing at things without permission

- interrupting others

- butting in or talking while others are talking

Ms. Lilly
SI Point to Ponder

Children watch every move you make. They learn to care about others by observing and experiencing the devotion of adult figures in their lives. Rejected children develop resiliency by connecting in meaningful and positive ways with the adults in their lives. Modeling is a powerful teaching tool. What are you modeling?

- pulling on teachers or peers while they are talking

- intruding on others' space without saying "Excuse me"

- bothering others who are trying to work

Encourage, model, and teach prosocial behavioral skills to assist a child in gaining entry into play with peers. Strategies to improve a rejected child's behaviors include the following.

PROVIDE LANGUAGE: Voice, emotion, timing, and tone are important social cues the child who is rejected needs to learn in order to become a better communicator and enter play with peers. Help the child set language goals and plan peer encounters to practice and achieve the objectives. For example, help the child plan a "meet and greet" script and rehearse how he might carry it out with a peer on the playground or during center time.

Here's a sample "meet and greet" script. Before playtime, practice the script with a child who has been rejected by his peers.

Child: "Hi, [insert other child's name]. Would you like to play with me?"

You: "What would you like to play?"

Child: "We could swing or play in the sand."

You: "Yes, I would like to play with you. Let's go swing!"

PLAY OUT SCENARIOS: Walk the child through the steps of the manners or outcomes desired. "This is how you ask a friend to play." "This is how you will gain my attention during class time." "This is how you will not attempt to gain my attention." Be as specific as possible, illustrating clearly what is acceptable and not acceptable. Practice over and over if needed.

COACH THROUGH AND MODEL MANNERS: Children may need coaching or modeling help with general manners, such as the following:

- Rejected children often disregard physical space boundaries when standing and speaking with others. They often intrude carelessly on others' personal space.

- Rejected children may need to be taught how to properly carry on a conversation while enjoying a snack with others.

Ms. Lilly
SI Point to Ponder

It is a rejected child who often needs her teacher the most. Constantly be on the lookout for possible reasons for a rejected child's behavior. When identified, teach the rejected child appropriate ways to express her needs and feelings. Develop plans to prevent problems—cut them off at the pass!

- Rejected children may need to be shown how to patiently wait for a turn.

- Rejected children may need to learn how to open doors for others, especially individuals with a disability.

REDIRECT ONCOMING POOR SOCIAL BEHAVIORS: Opportunities to teach social skills occur naturally in the classroom. When an opportunity presents itself, use redirection with positive reinforcement. For example, if you foresee a child attempting to throw a book angrily at a peer, redirect the behavior by having them sit with you and read the book together. Discuss respect for property with both children before reading the story. Ultimately, do not permit aggressive behavior. Respond immediately with nonaggressive body language.

Redirection is a powerful tool to defuse and address poor social skills and aggressive behavior. Taking turns and sharing are skills that often are problematic for children who have been rejected. Try using a visual cue to redirect or reinforce these skills. Here's a terrific game to underpin the concept. Playing the talking-stick game reinforces taking turns, sharing, and listening. Hold a stick and start telling a story. Then pass the stick on when it is time for another person to add to the story. The key is that the person with the stick is the only one allowed to talk. Enhance the activity by having the children make creative talking sticks out of a toilet paper tube or a thick branch. Decorate them artistically.

TEACH ENTRANCE STRATEGIES TO PLAY: Generally children learn to join play by watching and copying. They join right in, and most of the time they are readily accepted. Children who are rejected often find it difficult to join in or attempt to enter play. They need to learn and role-play entrance strategies. One suggestion is to teach these children how to gain entrance into play without the use of forceful, redundant questions or aggressive hovering around a play area. Model how to use kind and friendly words to gain entry into play instead of using unpredictable and overbearing body language.

WORK IN COOPERATIVE GROUPS: Working in cooperative groups is one of the best ways to address and treat struggling

Ms. Lilly
SI Play Tip

Young children require outdoor time for large-muscle activities and movement as well as for "brain breaks." Make it a point to get children outside daily for fresh air and sunshine. Even when the weather is nippy, being outdoors will benefit children's overall health and learning. Children who are rejected can often display rough and rowdy behaviors outdoors. Enforce these four "Rowdy Rules":
1. No kicking.
2. No hitting.
3. No pulling on clothes.
4. No hands on necks or over mouths.

social behaviors when using sensory-integration activities with rejected children. Children who are rejected often need help learning to read social cues, respond to their peers, share, and take turns. Working in cooperatives groups is beneficial for building such skills because fellow peers model proper behavior. Use positive and reinforcing words to teach children that their actions in group play have consequences; for example, "Sally, if you don't share the supplies, the group may not want to work with you again."

Teach a Rejected Child to Problem Solve

Children as young as three can be taught to resolve dilemmas in their play. The task can be challenging but is largely a matter of patience, delivery, and approach. Teaching a child who has been rejected to problem solve will also tremendously assist in the child's learning to read social cues, take turns, and wait.

MODEL "STICK-TO-ITIVENESS": Model how to handle frustration and how to persevere when something doesn't work right away. Use positive and encouraging words. Help the child see that it is okay to make mistakes. Expanded art projects or puzzles with many pieces are effective for teaching stick-to-itiveness.

TEACH FINDING ALTERNATIVES TO FRUSTRATING SITUATIONS ENCOUNTERED IN PLAY: Use flannelboards, puppets, or stories to walk a child through alternate ways to handle difficult social situations. "Charley, what else could you do if Johnny says he doesn't want to play with you? Let's think of ideas together. Maybe you could see if somebody else wants to play. Or come see me before you ask Johnny again. We could ask Johnny together."

TEACH HOW TO ANTICIPATE CONSEQUENCES: Role-play situations and incorporate creative strategies to teach the child that actions have consequences. Here's a yummy idea: Have the child and a few other classmates sort a variety of apples onto paper plates. Use Granny Smith, Red Delicious, Golden Delicious, Pink Lady, Jonathan, and Fuji apples. After all the apples are sorted, share and taste the different varieties.

Halfway through the activity, role-play what it would feel like if somebody didn't receive any apples or wasn't allowed to help sort them. Have the children anticipate the way it would make them feel to be left out and discuss how they would respond. "Why do you think Sarah is sad? Do you think it could be because we didn't let her help sort the apples?" Extend the anticipating consequences activity by helping children understand cause and effect within play. Role-play situations.

ROLE-PLAY SITUATIONS BEFORE SPECIFIC EVENTS: This is an excellent strategy to suggest to families. For example, if Christy is going to a birthday party, practice giving her friend the gift. Go over what she will say. Although simple sounding, it will make a big difference. In the classroom, practice verbal entrance strategies to play, such as "Veronica, that looks like a lot of fun. Can I play with you?" Discuss and role-play negotiating and compromising play situations as age appropriateness allows.

Ms. Lilly
SI Point to Ponder

Rejected children often attempt gaining attention or control of situations by verbally interrupting or physically barging into a play situation. This can turn into bullying. Children can't learn, play, or develop if they are scared of each other or feel unsafe in their environment. Physical bullying of any sort between children requires immediate attention.

Use the Three Cs: Be Calm, Clear, and Consistent

Children who are rejected usually require consistency. They thrive in a classroom with a calm teacher and with clear and consistent rules and routines. Children do not respond to yelling or negative reinforcement, so don't use it—it will get you nowhere fast! Stay calm and keep your body language nonaggressive and nonconfrontational.

Consistent routines and rules grant a sense of stability. Clear rules establish boundaries, respect for others, and health and safety guidelines. In addition to being clear, rules should be reasonable and explainable. Rejected children can benefit from understanding age-appropriate, realistic reasoning behind rules and limits. For example, "LaDonna, we use glue sticks during math time because glue sticks are not as messy as bottled glue. We use bottled glue for our art projects." Reinforcement of the three *Cs* will establish the trust and security that rejected children can use with your support to persevere during tough times.

Here are a few ideas to improve the three *Cs*—be calm, clear, and consistent:

- Post a child's daily schedule. Shoot for a sense of structure and purpose each day. If the child naps at noon, make sure the schedule denotes the time in a manner understandable to him. For preschoolers, putting pictures with a schedule is helpful. Suggest to families that schedules posted on a dry erase board work well at home too.

- A child who hears "No" a hundred times a day will eventually tune it out. Question what your "No" means. Is it wishy-washy or firm? Do children walk right over your "No," or do they know you mean business when you say it? Watch how you use it and look for opportunities to provide the child with a "Yes."

- Never compare children. Enough said.

An Individual Play Plan . . . for a Rejected Ricardo

See page 21 for a discussion about the rationale of an individual play plan. Developing an individual play plan for a rejected child will assist in guiding you to support, include, and review his strengths, needs, and current observable and measurable performance in the areas of play concern. An individual play plan is meant to help you decide which strategies to use and how best to adapt or modify them to suit the child and ultimately lessen the play challenge. A sample individual play plan for a rejected Ricardo follows.

INDIVIDUAL PLAY PLAN

Child's name: Ricardo
_____

Age: 6 years old
_____

Play challenge or concern:

Ricardo, a young ESL child, aggressively slaps his classmates to gain
their attention during play.

How does the play challenge affect involvement and progress in the general curriculum? For preschoolers and younger children, how does the play challenge affect involvement and progress in appropriate activities?

Ricardo's slapping has alienated him from many of his classmates during
play, causing detachment issues such as rejection.

Additional present levels of performance:

Ricardo's fine-motor skills (scissoring and using a pencil) are stagnant
from lack of involvement in center play and activities.

Sample goal, benchmark, or short-term objectives:

Ricardo will gently touch his classmates when wanting their attention,
as demonstrated, reminded, and modeled by his teacher.

Possible methods of measurement for Ricardo's goals:

• clinical observation of Ricardo's performance (Adult observation of
children is one of the most powerful assessment tools.)

• anecdotal notes about Ricardo

- checklists

- rating scales

- products (samples of what Ricardo has produced)

- portfolios (items selected over time to show progress)

- audio and video tapes

- photographs

- journals

- informal interviews

- conversations

- conferences with parents or guardians

Sensory-integration strategies and activities attempted (briefly respond to each play activity):

The following activities were attempted with Ricardo, who struggles to communicate with his playmates without aggressively slapping them.

Date: Feb 4 Activity: Redirect oncoming poor social behaviors (found on page 159)—Observation illustrated that using every opportunity available to redirect Ricardo's poor social skills is paying off.

Date: Feb 6 Activity: Play out scenarios (found on page 158)—Observations illustrated that playing out scenarios beforehand with Ricardo is helping him. Rehearsing what he may or may not say is a beneficial tool for Ricardo.

Selection of activity and how it has benefited the child:

The activities have benefited Ricardo, as he is no longer slapping his peers. Observation shows his classmates are warming up to him. They no longer forcibly express, "No, Ricardo, you can't play!"

Progress toward goals and objectives:

Ricardo no longer aggressively slaps his classmates to gain their attention during play.

Has the child's goal been met?

Ricardo's social skills are progressing. Continual modeling of how to gain his peers' attention, as demonstrated, reminded, and modeled by his teacher, is proving helpful. Ricardo's goal to gently touch his classmates when he wants their attention, as demonstrated, reminded, and modeled by his teacher, has not yet been met.

Notes and comments on regression/progression:

Ricardo no longer aggressively slaps his classmates to gain their attention during play. He currently resorts to raising his voice at them with his hands on his hips.

Wrapping Up

Children are drawn together by similarities. They are naturally curious creatures and enjoy making connections with one another. They easily notice individual differences as well, creating their own social curriculum guide. Learning social skills is a continual process, a process children who have been rejected often need support and guidance in mastering. When creating a productive environment for children who have been rejected by their peers, promote manners and respect for self and others. Ask yourself, "Does my curriculum emphasize play skills that incorporate kindness and empathy?" Make sure children who've been rejected don't feel threatened to lose control over their individual play. Use positive reinforcement when redirecting a child's blooming social skills. Be calm, clear, and consistent. These children need plenty of the three Cs with lots of unconditional love and patience inviting them openly to "Come and play!"

Check out the following resources for additional sensory-integration play ideas for children who are rejected.

Challenging Behavior in Young Children: Understanding, Preventing, and Responding Effectively by Barbara Kaiser and Judy Sklar Rasminsky

Kids Can Cooperate: A Practical Guide to Teaching Problem Solving by Elizabeth Crary

Pathways to Play! Combining Sensory Integration and Integrated Play Groups: Theme-Based Activities for Children with Autism Spectrum and Other Sensory-Processing Disorders by Glenda Fuge and Rebecca Berry

Appendix A

Early Childhood Social and Emotional Developmental Milestones List

Children's successful play skills should resemble the following by age eight. Use this list as a point of reference as you observe possible play challenges.

- interact with peers, showing an increasing ability to form friendships
- participate in cooperative play with one other child or more
- initiate interaction with peers and adults
- participate in cooperative play with one other child or more
- take turns appropriately
- share materials
- listen when others are speaking
- participate in back-and-forth peer conversation
- help each other figure things out
- use words, not inappropriate behavior, to express emotions
- follow rules
- seek to resolve conflict
- demonstrate self-regulation of behavior and emotions
- join other children in joint play, showing increasing ability to form friendships with several peers
- persist with a task
- remain focused
- work independently
- display impulse control
- present an appropriate self-concept
- identify self as part of a family and class unit
- engage in pretend play appropriately
- initiate communication to negotiate wants
- be aware of different emotions
- respond to different emotions
- be aware that personal actions have consequences

Appendix B

Blank Individual Play Plan

INDIVIDUAL PLAY PLAN

Child's name: _____

Age: _____

Play challenge or concern:

_____

_____

_____

How does the play challenge affect involvement and progress in the general curriculum? For preschoolers and younger children, how does the play challenge affect involvement and progress in appropriate activities?

_____

_____

_____

_____

Additional present levels of performance:

_____

_____

_____

Sample goal, benchmark, or short-term objectives:

_____

_____

_____

Possible methods of measurements for the child's goals:

• clinical observation of performance (Adult observation of children is one of the

   most powerful assessment tools.)

• anecdotal notes

• checklists

• rating scales

• products (samples of what the child produced)

• portfolios (items selected over time to show progress)

• audio and video tapes

• photographs

• journals

• informal interviews

• conversations

• conferences with parents or guardians

• _____

• _____

Sensory-integration strategies and activities attempted (briefly respond to each play activity):

_____

_____

_____

Date: _____ Activity: _____

_____

_____

Date: _____ Activity: _____

_____

_____

Selection of activity and how it has benefited the child:

_____

_____

_____

Progress toward goals and objectives:

_____

_____

_____

_____

Has the child's goal been met?

_____

_____

Notes and comments on regression/progression:

_____

_____

Appendix C

List of Creative Things to Use with Sensory-Integration Play Strategies

Please watch children closely at all times with all suggested materials. Older children can use items on the lists for younger children.

TWO TO THREE YEARS OF AGE

balls (various large sizes)
bandannas
baskets (all shapes, sizes, and textures)
blocks (large wooden and plastic)
bowls (plastic and all sizes)
bows (various colors)
boxes (all sizes)
cereal boxes
chalk (oversized for outdoors)
clay
clothes (old and oversized)
crates (plastic, milk)

cups (Dixie and Styrofoam)
dolls (all ethnic groups)
egg cartons
eye patches
funnels
gloves
hats
milk cartons or jugs
newspaper for crumpling
oatmeal boxes
pails
paper bags
paper plates (all sizes)
plastic containers (all sizes)

playdough
pots and pans (all sizes)
sand
shoe boxes
shovels
sponges (colored and larger sizes)
tires (clean; for climbing on)
tubs (plastic)
utensils (old, large kitchen)
wagons (for transporting dirt, sand, or "stuff")

FOUR TO FIVE YEARS OF AGE

beads
bottles of bubbles (tiny or blow size)
clothespins
cotton swabs
craft feathers
cupcake paper liners
envelopes
index cards
leaves (dry or fresh)
magazines
metal pie tins

mirrors (hand or full size)
outdated calendars
paintbrushes (all sizes)
paper (colored construction, card stock, computer, crepe . . . endless options)
pillowcases
pinecones
pipe cleaners/chenille stems
play money
postcards

ribbons
shoelaces
sponges (colored and all sizes)
spoons
straws (bendable)
string
toy people, animals, and vehicles
whistles
wooden craft sticks
yarn

SIX TO SEVEN YEARS OF AGE

acorns

aluminum foil

bottle caps

bouncy balls and jacks

bulk items from bargain bins after holidays (Halloween—face paint, fake fingernails; Valentine's Day—doilies, cards; Christmas—tiny Nutcracker soldiers, plastic ornaments)

buttons

cans

coat hangers (plastic)

coffee cans

counters (any small object that can be counted, sorted, or manipulated for classroom learning purposes: buttons, tiles, marbles, felt cutouts, nuts, seeds, dried beans, pasta, seashells)

film canisters

flowerpots

little candles for mud pies, clay cakes, or sand castle décor

miniature doll furniture

paper umbrellas (sold to put in beverages—clip sharp ends)

Ping-Pong balls

rubber bands

seeds

sequins

shells

spools (with or without thread)

toothpicks

"treasures" (polished stones, shells, jewels)

twisty ties

wallpaper scraps

Appendix D

Sample Parent Questionnaire

Dear Parent(s)/Guardian(s),

I look forward to a productive school year with your child. In an attempt to become better acquainted with him/her, I ask that you take a moment to answer the following questions. Doing so will help me cater specifically to your child's individual learning needs.

What interests your child?

_____

_____

_____

_____

What sort of activities does your child most enjoy?

_____

_____

What sort of activities does your child least enjoy?

_____

_____

Tell me about your child. What is his/her favorite color? Animal? What makes him/her special to you?

_____

_____

_____

_____

Does anything distract your child?

_____

_____

Where (in his/her room alone, at the kitchen table with you) and when (afternoon, evening) does your child work best?

_____

_____

About how long will your child focus (that is, what is your child's attention span)?

_____

_____

How would you describe your child's working pace?

_____

_____

How does your child like to learn? Using computers? Reading? Doing crafts? Hands-on activities?

_____

_____

I look forward to working together as a team to give your child a wonderful school year.

Thank you,

References

Bennett, Tess. 2006. Future teachers forge family connections. *Young Children* 61 (1): 22–27.

Biel, Lindsey, and Nancy Peske. 2005. *Raising a sensory smart child: The definitive handbook for helping your child with sensory integration issues.* New York: Penguin Group.

Bixler, Robert D., Myron E. Floyd, and William E. Hammutt. 2002. Environmental socialization: Qualitative tests of the childhood play hypothesis. *Environment and Behavior* 34 (6): 795–818.

Carlsson-Paige, Nancy, and Diane E. Levin. 1992. Making peace in violent times: A constructivist approach to conflict resolution. *Young Children* 48 (1): 4–13.

Christian, Linda Garris. 2006. Understanding families: Applying family systems theory to early childhood practice. *Young Children* 61 (1): 12–20.

Curtis, Deb, and Margie Carter. 2005. Rethinking early childhood environments to enhance learning. *Young Children* 60 (3): 34–38.

Dacey, John S., and Lisa B. Fiore. 2000. *Your anxious child: How parents and teachers can relieve anxiety in children.* San Francisco: John Wiley and Sons.

Dinwiddie, Sue A. 1994. The saga of Sally, Sammy, and the red pen: Facilitating children's social problem solving. *Young Children* 49 (5): 13–19.

Eliason, Claudia, and Loa Jenkins. 2003. *A practical guide to early childhood curriculum.* 7th ed. Upper Saddle River, NJ: Merrill Prentice Hall.

Elkind, David. 2007. *The power of play: How spontaneous, imaginative activities lead to happier, healthier, children.* Cambridge, MA: Da Capo Press.

Essa, Eva L., and Penelope Royce Rogers. 1992. *An early childhood curriculum: From developmental model to application.* Albany: Delmar.

Fjørtoft, Ingunn. 2001. The natural environment as a playground for children: The impact of outdoor play activities in pre-primary school children. *Early Childhood Education Journal* 29 (2): 111–17.

Grahn, Patrik, Fredrika Mårtensson, Bodil Llindbald, Paula Nilsson, and Anna Ekman. 1997. Ute pa Dagis. Stad and Land, 93/1991.

Herr, Judy. 1998. *Working with young children.* Tinley Park, IL: Goodheart-Wilcox Publisher.

Honig, Alice S. 2007. Play: Ten power boosts for children's early learning. *Young Children* 62 (5): 72–78.

Honig, Alice S., and Donna S. Wittmer. 1996. Helping children become more prosocial: Ideas for classrooms, families, schools, and communities. *Young Children* 51 (2): 62–70.

Humphryes, Janet. 2000. Exploring nature with children. *Young Children* 55 (2): 16–20.

Isbell, Christy, and Rebecca Isbell. 2007. *Sensory integration: A guide for preschool teachers.* Beltsville, MD: Gryphon House, Inc.

Katz, Lillian G., and Diane E. McClellan. 1997. *Fostering children's social competence: The teacher's role.* Washington DC: National Association for the Education of Young Children.

Kettman, Susan. 2005. *The 2,000 best games and activities: Using play to teach curiosity, self-control, kindness and other essential life skills.* Naperville, IL: Sourcebooks, Inc.

Kostelnik, Marjorie J. 1993. Recognizing the essentials of developmentally appropriate practice. *Child Care Information Exchange* 90 (3): 73–77.

Lamm, Sandra, Judith G. Groulx, Cindy Hansen, Mary Martin Patton, Anna Jimenez Slaton. 2006. Creating environments for peaceful problem solving. *Young Children* 60 (1): 22–27.

Laney, Marti Olsen. 2005. *The hidden gifts of the introverted child: Helping your child thrive in an extroverted world.* New York: Workman Publishing Company.

Louv, Richard. 2005. *Last child in the woods: Saving our children from nature-deficit disorder.* New York: Workman Publishing Company.

Luckey, Alicia J., and Richard A. Fabes. 2005. Understanding nonsocial play in early childhood. *Early Childhood Education Journal* 33 (2): 67–72.

Marcon, Rebecca A. 2003. Growing children: The physical side of development. *Young Children* 58 (1): 80–86.

Moore, Robin C. 1986. The power of nature orientations of girls and boys toward biotic and abiotic play settings on a reconstructed schoolyard. *Children's Environmental Quarterly* 3 (3): 52–69.

———. 1996. Compact nature: The role of playing and learning gardens on children's lives. *Journal of Therapeutic Horticulture* 8, 72–82.

Petty, Karen. 2009. Using guided participation to support young children's social development. *Young Children* 64 (4): 80–85.

Ramsey, Robert D. 2003. *501 tips for teachers.* New York: McGraw-Hill.

Rogers, Liz, and Dana Steffan. 2009. Clay play. *Young Children* 60 (1): 22–27.

Schirrmacher, Robert. 2002. *Art and creative development for young children.* Albany: Delmar, Thomson Learning.

Sher, Barbara. 2004. *Smart play: 101 fun, easy games that enhance intelligence.* Hoboken, NJ: John Wiley and Sons.

Van Hoorn, Judith, Patricia Monighan Nourat, Barbara Scales, and Keith Rodriquez Alward. 2003. *Play at the center of the curriculum.* 3rd ed. Upper Saddle River, NJ: Prentice Hall.

Ward, Christina D. 1996. Adult Intervention: Appropriate Strategies for Enriching the Quality of Children's Play. *Young Children* 51 (3): 20–26.

Wells, Nancy M., and Gary W. Evans. 2003. Nearby nature: A buffer of life stress among rural children. *Environment and Behavior* 35 (3): 311–30.

Wilson, Ruth A. 1997. The wonders of nature: Honoring children's ways of knowing. *Early Childhood News* 9 (2): 6–9, 16–19.